Dear Hope:

encouragement for
project. hopefully b...
time this arrives comps hell
will be over. Congrats, my
friend!

HAPPY NEW YEAR '02!
Love,
Roz

52 McGs.

The Best Obituaries
from Legendary *New York Times* Writer
Robert McG. Thomas Jr.

EDITED BY

Chris Calhoun

FOREWORD BY

Thomas Mallon

SCRIBNER

NEW YORK   LONDON   TORONTO   SYDNEY   SINGAPORE

For Joan Thomas

SCRIBNER
1230 Avenue of the Americas
New York, NY 10020

SCRIBNER and design are trademarks of Macmillan Library Reference USA, Inc.,
used under license by Simon & Schuster, the publisher of this work.

DESIGNED BY ERICH HOBBING

Text set in New Caledonia

Manufactured in the United States of America

1   3   5   7   9   10   8   6   4   2

Library of Congress Cataloging-in-Publication Data

Thomas, Robert McG. (Robert McGill).
52 McGs.: the best obituaries from legendary New York Times writer Robert McG.
Thomas Jr. / edited by Chris Calhoun; foreword by Thomas Mallon.
p. cm.
1. Biography—20th century. 2. Obituaries. 3. Celebrities—Biography.
I. Title: Fifty-two McGs. II. Calhoun, Chris. III. Title.
CT120 .T46 2001
920.073—dc21   2001042952

ISBN 0-7432-1562-1

CONTENTS

FOREWORD

It is amazing how many of these you will remember.

You first read them with your morning coffee, or on the subway, or waiting for the computer to boot up—always while you were moving headlong into another day of busy and ordinary *life*. And yet they stuck, to the mind and heart. During the last half of the 1990s, the obits became a must-read for thousands of New Yorkers who let the latest doings of Bill Clinton and Rudy Giuliani wait a few minutes, until they had found out what Charles McCartney ("Known for Travels with Goats") and Angelo Zuccotti ("Artist of the Velvet Rope") had been up to all their lives. Of an art that stretches from Milton to the webmasters of *Good Bye!*, the on-line "Journal of Contemporary Obituaries," Robert McG. Thomas Jr. (1939–2000) was the modern and too short-lived American master.

A lover of the far-fetched and the overlooked, he reveled in making sure that even in the Newspaper of Record, the last could be first. Assigned to the obits desk in 1995, after a long *Times* career that took him from copyboy up through the sports and society sections, the burly six-foot-four Thomas was ready to escort a parade of eccentrics and unknowns through a needle's eye toward improbable fame and, for all one knows, heaven. His send-offs were funny, stylish and unfailingly soulful. He could be a New Orleans jazz band or a hushed friar as occasion demanded and always, unbelievably enough, on the pages of *The New York Times*.

Luckily enough, the paper—in particular, editor Marvin Siegel—realized what it had in Thomas. "They learned to assign him the disenfranchised," says Bill Brink, his friend and onetime colleague on the sports desk. The paper also let him rearrange

7

the obituary's hitherto rigid formulae and put him to work more often on deadline than in advance. "If they didn't give him something until three o'clock, they'd have something great by eight," says Brink.

"Philip O'Connor, an incorrigible, flamboyant and decidedly self-absorbed British eccentric who turned a fulsomely frank account of his abject childhood and misspent youth into a rollicking literary sensation in 1958, died on Friday at his home near Uzes in southern France." Every lead was the subject's life. Thomas had to keep syntax steady and see things whole, get the corpse across the Styx and into the reader's field of vision—to say nothing of his weekday-morning attention span. In a genre that requires cramming, he never seems rushed. He could get things done with the confident simplicity of Trollope. "Mr. Anderson, a bachelor, was rich as well as lonely"—thus is an ex-slave and old soldier readied for his marriage to Miss Daisy Graham, the subject of the first piece in this collection. (It's no wonder Thomas did Maurice Sagoff proud on March 29, 1998, commemorating the art of another compressor who had reduced the plot of *Crime and Punishment* to twenty short lines of verse.)

Thomas had dozens of playful tricks that, in the end, the *Times*'s editors decided could safely be used upon the obscure departed if not the living luminaries of the A section. If they hadn't been dead already, Thomas might have killed some of his subjects with his puns; and he could parody with the best. About Anne Hummert, the creator of over a dozen soap operas, he asked: "Can a career woman who sacrificed her leisure to keep a nation of enthralled housewives glued to their radios for the better part of two decades survive a heart-wrenching regimen of producing as many as 90 cliff-hanging episodes a week to live a full, rich and long life?" Beautifully alert to verbs—"Hal Lipset, a storied San Francisco sleuth who helped elevate, or rather reduce, electronic surveillance to a miniature art"—Thomas wrote as if he'd never heard of an exclamation point, let alone thought of using one. In his hands, irony was not the all-pervasive, self-congratulatory thing it is today. He loved it for its funny, cosmic consolations: Sidney Korshak, the lawyer-fixer, "became so valuable to the mob and its corrupt union allies that lower-level mobsters were ordered never to approach him, lest they tarnish his reputation for trust and integrity."

In an era of bloated life-writing, Thomas restored the biographical essay. Try to cut almost any of the pieces in this volume and you'll be cutting, in more than one sense, into bone. One doubts, however, that this grand obituarist would have made a good book-length biographer. Like Hal Lipset, the electronic eavesdropper, Thomas was a natural miniaturist. Full-blown biography would have required him to situate, evaluate and categorize—to take the long, chronological view when he was so much inclined to the shapely, enthusiastic burst. Besides, he probably never would have finished the book. A literary agent once approached him to do a life of Jack Kerouac, and "the way he reacted was typical," recalls Bill Brink, now the *Times's* deputy sports editor. "He went out and bought fifteen books by and about Kerouac. He plunged in and then never got around to the proposal."

The pages that follow are full of wit and without a trace of snideness. When Thomas needs to debunk—say, the claim that Walter J. Kuron flew in the Red Baron's flight wing—he does the job with an almost regretful gentleness. He never condescends, especially to the kind. The Mormons who sew mittens for people with AIDS are "elderly volunteers for whom the familiar act of knitting or crocheting became a way to relate to a baffling world beyond their experience." And the Reverend Louis A. Saunders is celebrated as a fellow artist of concision for "one of the briefest eulogies ever: 'Mrs. Oswald tells me that her son, Lee Harvey, was a good boy and that she loved him. And today, Lord, we commit his spirit to Your divine care.'"

Thomas loved oddball information for its own sake, but one shouldn't ignore the casual, inductive education so many of these pieces provide without even trying. An obit for R. V. Patwardhan, the Manhattan Hindu priest who modified the incendiary portion of his faith's wedding ceremony to conform to New York's fire laws, brings to life the beginnings of a whole community prior to a sea change in immigration law. Similarly, Thomas's treatment of Sydney Guilaroff, "Stylist to the Stars," shows him playing both the white and black keys with a lovely lack of strain; a man, a milieu and an era are unrolled in twelve harmonious bars.

Thomas did not need a subject's life to be "crowded with incident," as Lady Bracknell once put it. He was more intrigued by accident—Edward Lowe's now legendarily fortuitous discovery of Kitty Litter, or the way Fred Feldman became a helicopter traffic reporter. He was especially pleased if the unexpected occurrence had led the subject into a lifetime of doing what he loved. Versatility did not impress RMcGT Jr.; being steadily tickled by something did: Milton Rubincam's genealogy; Toots Barger's championship duckpins-playing; Francine Katzenbogen's cats. Thomas loved charming inanities—the state sport of Maryland is jousting, not duckpins—and people who are, above all, harmless, a human condition far rarer than one might think.

The photographer Alfred Eisenstaedt once told me that he didn't like "gruesome" pictures, but the sunniness of his art proved no impediment to his becoming one of the twentieth-century's most vivid chroniclers. Thomas, too, didn't relish unpleasant subject matter: his obituary of Nguyen Ngoc Loan, famous for executing a Viet Cong prisoner with a shot to the head in exactly the kind of photo Eisie disliked, is wisely included here, even though the piece is not one of Thomas' best. A reader can tell that his heart isn't in it.

He was better let loose upon the odd and the humble. His best, most talked-about obits, in the sort of paradox he relished, gave relief from the 1990s culture of celebrity. In fact, if Thomas had come upon the same epitaph that Hawthorne once spotted in the Lillington churchyard—

> Poorly lived,
> And poorly died,
> Poorly buried,
> And no one cried

—I suspect he would have taken the words as a challenge to his profession and, perhaps, his soul.

"He singlehandedly humanized the paper," says Michael T. Kaufman, another friend and *Times* colleague, to whom fell the truly unenviable task of writing an obituary for Thomas himself.

He is survived by everyone he ever wrote about. If you still can't take it with you, you can now—thanks to his fan and posthumous editor, Chris Calhoun—take up, once more, with several dozen personalities that Thomas, on deadline, brought to life. "He was a bon vivant," remembers Bill Brink, "who would literally grab people in the elevators or lobby to get them to go to dinner. We'd start out as a twosome and end up as five." At the restaurant, "he'd put together the most eclectic table arrangements, pretty young girls next to grizzled newspapermen." Like his ultimate employer, Death, he was a great leveler.

Reader, consider yourself grabbed. You're off to a marvelous party, and Robert McG. Thomas Jr. is still the life of it.

THOMAS MALLON

EDITOR'S NOTE

My efforts to get this little book published were for the most part selfish. My clippings of *New York Times* obituaries written by Robert McG. Thomas Jr. were unorganized and disintegrating. Some were tucked into books, several sat in various desk drawers, others rested on my kitchen table yellowing next to a stack of bills. One summer day, I found a well-worn obit of Patsy Southgate in the glove box of my old Cutlass and reread it with delight while passing through a car wash.

Missing Thomas's byline for several weeks that same summer, I asked around and learned he was away from work, fighting cancer. I had never met him, but wrote him a fan letter and get-well note introducing myself. I explained that my friends and I adored his stories of the recently dead, even collected them and passed them around, that we called them McGs. and missed him every day.

I was hoping to hear back from Thomas but knew I never would when I read with sadness Michael Kaufman's obituary of him in the *Times* of January 8, 2000 (brilliantly McG-ish in its own right, it is included at the end of this book). Several weeks later I was amazed to learn from a friend that my letter was read at his memorial service. Later still, I was told by his son, David, that the letter had hung on the wall of his hospital room. Thrilled to know Thomas had received my note, I pondered the nice irony of this last minute connection with the man I so admired for the connections he made with the dead.

After transferring to the *Times* obit desk full time, Thomas wrote a total of 657 McGs. From that lot, with a couple of early exceptions, I have chosen these fifty-two to show Thomas at his coolest, corniest, smartest, sweetest and all-time greatest. Naturally, it was difficult to limit the selection and exclude over six hundred pieces—all true McGs.—but I liked the sound of fifty-two, and that is enough, I think, for a good sample of his ungovernable range. Plus, I want to suggest that the reader need not approach the book in the usual front-to-back way but can proceed randomly as one would pick a card, any card, from a deck. A loaded deck, however, for these are all aces.

I would like to thank Judy Greenfeld, Linda Lake, Marvin Siegel, Phyllis Collazo and especially Mike Levitas at *The New York Times* for their time and generosity. Thanks to my friends Rick Woodward and Christine Buckley, who helped me with selecting and confirming the choices, and to Tom Mallon for his wonderful foreword. Thanks also to Mary Beth Keane and Rachel Sussman, who were instrumental to this project, and to Bob Thomas's friends Bob Grossman, Bill Brink and Michael Kaufman for their encouragement and kindness. Finally, without the vision and wisdom of Gillian Blake, senior editor at Scribner, there would be no book. I thank her the most.

CHRIS CALHOUN

52 McGs.

Daisy Anderson, 97,

Widow of Former Slave

and Union Soldier

Daisy Anderson, an old man's darling who kept the flame of her own youthful love and her husband's searing slave memories burning for more than three quarters of a century, died last Saturday at a nursing home in Denver. She was 97, and, as the oldest of the nation's three known surviving Civil War widows, may also have been the last widow of a Southern slave.

The death of Miss Daisy, as she was known, leaves only two known surviving widows of Civil War veterans, one each from the Union and Confederate armies.

One, Alberta Martin, 91, of Elba, Ala., whose husband fought for the South, joined Miss Daisy at a ceremony at Gettysburg last year. The other, Gertrude Grubb Janeway, 89, of Blaine, Tenn., is the widow of a Union soldier.

No official records exist of the marital histories of former slaves, but the arithmetic suggesting that Miss Daisy may have been the last woman married to a man born into Southern bondage is compelling.

When they were married in Forest City, Ark., in 1922, Miss Daisy was 21, and her husband, Robert Anderson, was 79.

For Miss Daisy, or Daisy Graham, a native of Hardin County, Tenn., whose impoverished sharecropping family had moved to Arkansas because of racial tensions when she was 17, it was hardly love at first sight.

When she first saw Mr. Anderson, in church, she recalled snickering at the sight of his bushy white beard.

But Mr. Anderson, who was born into slavery in Green County, Ky., in 1843 and grew up on a flax and hemp plantation before fleeing with his master's blessing to join the Union Army in the waning days of the Civil War in 1865, had more than whiskers to offer the lithe young woman who eked out a living teaching the alphabet to neighborhood children and owned one dress.

Mr. Anderson, who saw no action in the Civil War but later took part in the western Indian campaigns, had done well since being mustered out of the Army in 1867.

After several abortive farming ventures he had acquired a 2,000-acre homestead in Nebraska and made such a success of it that by the time he visited a brother in Forest City in 1922, Mr. Anderson, a bachelor, was rich as well as lonely.

Whatever her reaction to his whiskers, once Mr. Anderson began talking about his experiences as a slave, soldier and gentleman farmer, Miss Daisy was captivated.

Thirty days after being introduced by a matchmaking preacher, they were married and began what Miss Daisy later described as an eight-year honeymoon, which ended when her husband was killed in an automobile accident in 1930.

Mr. Anderson took his bride on an extensive trip through the West and lavished her with clothes and other gifts. The gifts continued after they settled on his ranch, which she recalled had 20 hands and two cooks.

He also regaled his wife with stories of his childhood as a slave, so impressing her that she turned them into a book, "From Slavery to Affluence: Memoirs of Robert Anderson, Ex-Slave," which was published privately in 1927.

After her husband's death, Miss Daisy, who said she had been spoiled by his generosity, became such a spendthrift that she soon lost the farm in the Depression.

After that she had a largely hardscrabble life, joining a sister in Steamboat Springs, Colo., and eventually acquiring a 10-acre farm in nearby Strawberry Park, where she raised geese and chickens, kept a garden, ran a restaurant with a sister and worked as a guide.

For all the drama of her own life, Miss Daisy, who lectured widely in her later years, becoming such a celebrity that she was introduced to Pope John Paul II in Denver in 1993 and presented President Clinton with a copy of her book there last year, made it her life's mission to work for racial harmony and keep the memory of her husband alive.

Originally named after his owner, Col. Robert Ball, Mr. Anderson, who never saw his mother after she was sold to a Louisiana sugar plantation when he was 6, later adopted the name Anderson after the neighboring farmer who owned his father.

Although he always described his own master as kind, Mr. Anderson suffered horribly at the hands of the man's third wife, a drunken harridan who once gave him a savage rawhide whipping, then rubbed salt and black pepper into his wounds, leaving such extensive scars that Miss Daisy later said the welts on his back were as thick as her own fingers.

She was in a position to know. She had lovingly used her own fingers to trace the very scars of slavery and had vowed that they would not be forgotten.

Miss Daisy, who never remarried and had no children, is survived by two nieces, Mary L. Cox of Westminster, Colo., and Anne Williams of Los Angeles.

September 26, 1998

Lewis J. Gorin Jr.,

Instigator of a 1930's Craze,

Dies at 84

Lewis J. Gorin Jr., a Princeton-educated, Harvard-trained lawyer who had a long, respectable and thoroughly obscure career as a business executive, gentleman farmer and amateur military historian, died on Jan. 1 at his home in Louisville, Ky. He was 84 and all but forgotten as the man who had tickled a dispirited nation's funny bone in 1936 with a tongue-in-cheek tour de force that created a brushfire national student movement and made Mr. Gorin the most famous collegian in America who did not actually play football.

If Mr. Gorin's 1936 achievement is hardly remembered, there is a reason. For if fame is fleeting, so is innocence, and World War II is no longer the laughing matter it could still be in March 1936, when as a Princeton senior Mr. Gorin founded and became the first national commander of the Veterans of Future Wars, an organization formed expressly to obtain an immediate $1,000 bonus for each of the 15 million young Americans who were sure to serve in a war that had not even started.

As Mr. Gorin deadpanned at the time, with war in Europe clearly imminent and with eventual American involvement a foregone conclusion, the future veterans wanted their bonuses while they were still young and healthy enough to enjoy them—and (as he made clear in a follow-up satiric book, "Prepaid Patriotism," published two months later) while the nation still had enough money to pay them before greedy World War I veterans succeeded in squeezing the country dry.

At a time when there was widespread resentment against the American Legion and the Veterans of Foreign Wars for having browbeaten Congress into passing, over President Franklin D. Roosevelt's veto, $2 billion in accelerated bonuses for 4 million World War I veterans, most of whom had never made it beyond stateside training camps, Mr. Gorin's inspired spoof had far-reaching resonance.

Mr. Gorin, who said he got the idea while drinking tea at a campus coffee shop, had no intention of forming an actual organization until a friend, Robert G. Barnes, bet him $5 that he could get the group national publicity if it had a program. Mr. Barnes, who happened to be the campus correspondent for The New York Times and The Associated Press, won the bet.

Within days after Mr. Gorin, Mr. Barnes and a handful of others had founded the organization and published a manifesto in the student newspaper on March 16, the movement had generated reams of headlines, spread to scores of campuses across the country, enlisted tens of thousands of members, and spawned a women's auxiliary, the Association of Future Gold Star Mothers. Instead of bonuses, the women demanded free trips to Europe to view the future graves of their unborn sons.

Catching the spirit, students elsewhere added wrinkles. At Rensselaer Polytechnic Institute, Future Profiteers demanded advances on future war contracts, and Sweetbriar College students formed a chapter of Future Golddiggers "to sit on the laps of future profiteers while they drink champagne during the next war."

Not everyone was amused. James E. Van Zandt, national commander of the Veterans of Foreign Wars, denounced the Gorin group as "a bunch of monkeys," and declared they would never be veterans because they were "too yellow to go to war."

Like others, including some who saw the Veterans of Future Wars as pacifists and others who viewed them as communists, Mr. Van Zandt missed the point.

A descendant of the Revolutionary War general Artemus Ward and a man who was later active in the Sons of the American Revolution, the Society of the Colonial Wars and the Society of the Cincinnati, Mr. Gorin saw himself as the consummate patriot, one who would willingly answer his country's call in time of war, accept his soldier's pay, then return to civilian life without feeling entitled to further feedings at the public trough.

By the fall of 1936, with Mr. Gorin at Harvard, the country distracted by a Presidential campaign and the gifts that had kept the group's headquarters humming now drying up, the joke was over. The Veterans of Future Wars suspended operations, revoking the charters of 500 posts across the country.

Four years later, as a young lawyer in Louisville, Mr. Gorin was among 21 civic leaders who signed an ad calling for an end to American neutrality laws that blocked aid to allies.

As he had expected, when the United States did go to war, Mr. Gorin, along with the vast majority of the former Veterans of Future Wars, went with it, serving as an artillery captain in Italy, France and Germany and later writing and publishing "The Cannon's Mouth," a history of field artillery in World War II.

After the war, he accepted an offer from a childhood friend, Billy Reynolds, to join the family's aluminum company, Reynolds Metals, and became an executive with its international subsidiary, first in Louisville, where he made an abortive run for Congress in the 1950's, later in Bermuda and ultimately in Richmond, Va.

After his retirement in 1981, he returned to Louisville, operated a farm in southern Kentucky and continued to amuse his friends with his geniality and once-renowned wit.

Mr. Gorin is survived by his wife, Eleanor; a daughter, Eleanor Leuenberger of Schlossrued, Switzerland; a son, Jeff of Tempe, Ariz.; a brother, Standiford of McMinnville, Tenn., and five grandchildren.

January 31, 1999

Ted Hustead Is Dead at 96;
Built the Popular Wall Drug

Anybody who watched Ted Hustead roll into Wall, S.D., on a cattle truck in December 1931, his wife and 4-year-old son at his side, the family's entire stock of meager possessions piled in the back, would have needed quite a crystal ball to predict that by the time Mr. Hustead died two-thirds of a century later, the governor of South Dakota would be moved to open his annual state-of-the-state address with a tribute to the man who became a beloved South Dakota legend by turning a small-town pharmacy named Wall Drug into the world's most popular drugstore.

A sprawling tourist attraction of international renown, it takes in more than $10 million a year and draws some two million annual visitors to a remote town whose population has never risen above 800.

Then again, hot, dusty and remote as Wall was and is, 50 miles east of Rapid City on the edge of the notorious Badlands, not even Mr. Hustead could have predicted just how far a pharmacist could go—or how far people would travel to come to him—with the offer of a free drink of ice water and a ubiquitous, world-famous network of clever roadside signs and bumper stickers.

Or as Gov. William J. Janklow put it on Wednesday, a day after Mr. Hustead died at 96 at a hospital in Philip, S.D.: "He's a guy that figured out that free ice water could turn you into a phenomenal success in the middle of a semi-arid desert way out in the middle of someplace."

Or nowhere, as it seemed at the time.

Certainly, in 1931 it would have been hard to predict that anyone who settled in Wall would make much of a mark, let alone a 28-year-old pharmacist who had used the entire $3,000 he inherited from his father to buy the town's lone drug store.

A doctor's son from Phillips, Neb., Mr. Hustead had earned a pharmacist's degree from the University of Nebraska and worked as a farm laborer and later at a grain elevator in Sioux Falls before heeding his mother's advice to seek independence.

According to family lore, as the truck made the 300-mile trek to Wall, the driver described the rigors of the West with such mounting fervor and in such vivid detail that by the time he got around to the snakes, little Billy was so distraught he asked why in the world the family had left its nice little brick house in Sioux Falls for such a forsaken place.

"Because," his mother, Dorothy, explained, "your father is crazy."

Settling in the store's back room, the Husteads agreed to stick it out for five years, but after taking in only $360 the first month and not much more after that, it began to seem that Wall Drug had been a dead end.

Then, with only six months to go on the five-year limit and just after the family had moved to a house out near the highway, Mrs. Hustead had a brainstorm.

Going home for a nap on an especially hot Sunday in July 1936, she was back in an hour complaining that she hadn't been able to sleep because of the incessant rumble of traffic on Route 16.

It got her to thinking, she said, that if they put up a little sign out on the highway offering free ice water to tourists on their way to Mount Rushmore maybe some of them would turn off to quench their thirst and perhaps even buy something.

Inspired by the proliferating Burma Shave ditties of the day, she even composed a little jingle: "Get a soda / Get root beer / Turn next corner / Just as near / To Highway 16 and 14 / Free Ice Water / Wall Drug."

Mr. Hustead needed no further prodding. By the time he got back from putting up the sign the next day, cars had already started turning off and making the block and a half to Wall Drug on Main Street.

They haven't stopped. Fired by the initial success, Mr. Hustead began expanding the store, adding wares and attractions while installing signs along every highway in South Dakota and neighboring states, all proclaiming just how much farther a motorist had to go to reach the promised land of Wall Drug.

In time Mr. Hustead was spending $300,000 a year on billboard advertising, including Wall Drug signs on London buses and in every train station in Kenya. But it was American G.I.'s who took up the craze and spread the Wall Drug word to the far corners of the world. During World War II it seemed that every sign saying "Kilroy was here," was accompanied by one giving the mileage to Wall Drug.

(Regulations to keep the nation's scenic highways free of visual pollution eventually crimped the Hustead style. Still, after I-90 replaced the old highways, periodic surveys showed that as much as three-quarters of the traffic turned off to visit Wall Drug, but then who can resist an exit marked by an 80-foot dinosaur?)

In addition to delighting motorists, the signs generated hundreds of newspaper and magazine articles, many displayed on a wall of Wall Drug, a tourist attraction that seems famous largely for its very fame.

Today, even after the little store has been expanded into a 75,000-square-foot colossus of western kitsch with an enclosed mall, dozens of shops selling everything from T-shirts to expensive boots (you can have wine with your buffalo burger in the 400-plus-seat restaurant), a summertime staff of 250 and an array of corny free attractions like a cowboy orchestra that plays every 15 minutes, the quintessential way to experience Wall Drug seems to be to stand at the wall of clippings reading about people standing at the wall of clippings reading about people standing at the wall.

Long after he turned over active management to his son, Bill, whose recent illness has forced him to hand the reins to his sons, Rick and Ted, the proprietor was a constant, proud presence at Wall Drug.

Mr. Hustead, whose wife died in 1994, and whose survivors include another son, Charles of Topeka, Kan.; two daughters, Mary Bottum and Catherine Roe, both of Los Angeles; 17 grandchildren and 22 great-grandchildren, knew that there were other popular international tourist attractions.

The Taj Mahal, for example. As the sign says, it's "only 10,728 miles to Wall Drug."

January 17, 1999

Jesse Hill Ford, 66,
a Novelist Who Wrote
of Race Relations

Jesse Hill Ford, the novelist whose haunting examination of the destructive relations between the races in his native South helped sow the seeds of destruction of his own acclaimed literary career, took his life on Saturday at his home in Nashville. He was 66 and had undergone open heart surgery six weeks ago.

His friend and biographer, Anne Cheney, said Mr. Ford, who had become depressed since the apparently successful surgery, had locked himself in his library and shot himself in the head.

A native of Troy, Ala., who grew up in Nashville, studied with the Fugitive poet Donald Davidson at Vanderbilt University and later with the Fugitive writer Andrew Lytle at the University of Florida, Mr. Ford seemed destined to take his place among the pantheon of Southern writers.

After serving as a Navy officer in the Korean War and spending a couple of years in public relations, he married his college sweetheart and settled down in the west Tennessee town of Humboldt to write full time.

Although he wrote dozens of short stories and several screenplays, it was the second of his four novels, "The Liberation of Lord Byron Jones," published by Atlantic–Little Brown in 1965, that established his reputation.

The novel, whose richly detailed characters range from starry-eyed white liberals to lynch-law throwbacks and an array of black and white characters caught between their competing sensibilities, is the story of a prosperous black undertaker who is so determined to obtain a just, dignified divorce from his philandering young wife that he insists on naming a white policeman as her lover. When the undertaker's prominent white lawyer feels compelled to alert the policeman to his client's intentions, the policeman murders the undertaker.

The book won wide acclaim, became a best seller and made Mr. Ford wealthy, but it did not make him popular in Humboldt. His neighbors, who knew that the novel was based on actual people and events, felt betrayed, especially after a 1970 William Wyler movie starring Lee J. Cobb, Roscoe Lee Browne, Lola Falana and Anthony Zerbe gave the story even wider circulation.

Mr. Ford, whose next novel, "The Feast of St. Barnabas" (1969), also dealt with racial conflict, said that he and his family received numerous threats, mainly from white residents of Humboldt. But when black players were barred from the high school football team in the wake of the integration of the town's school system, Mr. Ford's son, the team captain, began to receive threats from black people.

It was against that backdrop that Mr. Ford, seeing a strange car drive up and park on the grassy shoulder of his private driveway one night in 1970, left his house with a rifle and fired two shots, killing the driver, a black soldier who had apparently chosen the remote spot only for a romantic interlude with his girlfriend.

Mr. Ford, who said he was afraid that the man had parked there to ambush his son, insisted that the killing was an accident, that he had not aimed at the driver but had fired impulsively only to hold the car there until the police arrived.

Much to the glee of many of his Humboldt neighbors, he was charged with murder. The 1971 trial drew widespread national attention, and although he was found not guilty, many believed that Mr. Ford had been the beneficiary of the very brand of distorted Southern justice he had exposed so vividly in his novel.

"I don't think he ever recovered from the trial," said Ms. Cheney, an associate professor of English at Virginia Tech whose biography, "The Life and Letters of Jesse Hill Ford, Southern Writer," has just been published by Edwin Mellen. "It took everything he had in him to finish 'The Raider.' "

After that novel was published in 1975, he never wrote another.

His last published writings startled those who had known Mr. Ford as a committed liberal. As a guest columnist for USA Today in 1989 and 1990 he emerged as a crotchety, outspoken conservative who defended Oliver L. North, railed against the American Civil Liberties Union and said flag burners should have their heads broken.

Mr. Ford is survived by his wife, Lillian; four children from his previous marriage, Jon Jr. of Jackson, Tenn., Charles of Steamboat Springs, Colo., Sara Langley of Bells, Tenn., and Elizabeth Hohenberg of Memphis; a sister, Ann Sellers of Syracuse, and eight grandchildren.

June 5, 1996

Anne Hummert, 91, Dies;

Creator of Soap Operas

Faithful followers of soap operas have learned over the years that after a brief and bitter first marriage a young single mother can find love, marriage and singular professional success with a much older man, but now the question is:

Can a career woman who sacrificed her leisure to keep a nation of enthralled housewives glued to their radios for the better part of two decades survive a heart-wrenching regimen of producing as many as 90 cliff-hanging episodes a week to live a full, rich and long life?

No need to stay tuned or wait for a toothpaste commercial. It can now be revealed that when she died in bed at her Fifth Avenue apartment on July 5, Anne Hummert, the woman widely credited with creating the radio soap opera and spinning out many of the classics of the 1930's and 40's, was a 91-year-old multimillionaire who had maintained a vigorous life almost to the end.

At a time when televised soap operas have become a postfeminist cultural sideshow, it is hard to imagine the era when "Stella Dallas," "Helen Trent," "Ma Perkins" and "Lorenzo Jones" were more than household names, and when virtually every woman in America knew that Mary Noble was the "Backstage Wife" and were familiar with every detail of the anguished but inspiring lives of "John's Other Wife" and "Young Widow Brown."

It is even harder to imagine that all of these plus more than a dozen others were the creations of a diminutive dynamo from Baltimore and the man she kept at bay for seven years after taking a job as his assistant at a Chicago advertising agency.

By the time she met E. Frank Hummert in 1927, the former Anne Schumacher had lived something of a soap opera herself. A brilliant student who graduated magna cum laude from Goucher College at age 20 in 1925, she had begun her career as a college correspondent for The Sun, then worked as a Sun reporter before going to Paris in 1926.

She became a reporter for the precursor of The International Herald Tribune her first day in the city, but within a year she had married and divorced a fellow reporter, John Ashenhurst, and was back in the United States with an infant son.

Settling in Chicago, she failed to get a newspaper job but became an assistant to Mr. Hummert, a former St. Louis newspaperman who had become a renowned copywriter and a partner in the Chicago agency Blackett, Sample & Hummert.

He was some two decades older than she and a confirmed bachelor, but then he had never met a woman quite like his captivating 22-year-old assistant with the tinkling voice, who was such a fount of ideas and organized efficiency that she became a vice president just two years later.

She, on the other hand, had already been married to one newspaperman, thank you, and was in no hurry to marry another. The couple didn't marry until 1934, when they began what friends recall as one of the great love matches, which lasted until Mr. Hummert's death in 1966.

At a time when commercial programming in the infant medium concentrated on working people who returned home to sit in front of their radios at night, advertisers were dimly aware that the housewives who stayed home all day were the nation's primary purchasing agents. But these women were considered too busy to pay more than cursory attention to the family radio.

The Hummerts didn't argue with the theory of the distracted housewife. They simply seized her attention and changed the pattern of her life. After "Just Plain Bill" hit the daytime airwaves in 1933, housewives arranged their work so they would never miss an episode of the small-town barber who married above himself.

Although a short-lived 1930 program, "Painted Lives" by Irna Phillips, is regarded as the first radio soap opera, it was "Just Plain Bill," which began at night in 1932, that created the cultural juggernaut that would eventually be nicknamed for the product that often sponsored it.

Within months the show had spawned many copycats, few as successful as those turned out by the Hummerts themselves, who had as many as 18 separate 15-minute serials running at a time for a total of 90 episodes a week, each ending with an unresolved crisis that was heightened for the Friday episode.

The couple, who formed their own company, Hummert Productions, and moved to New York in the mid-1930's, farmed out the writing after they had dreamed up the original idea and mapped out the initial story line. But they were deeply involved in every aspect of each production, from casting to script editing.

Mrs. Hummert, who had a photographic memory, was renowned in the industry for her ability to remember each intricate twist of every one of their creations.

It was a reflection of the grip the Hummerts had on their audience that their programs generated more than five million letters a year, and it was a measure of their commercial success that by 1939 Hummert programs accounted for more than half the advertising revenues generated by daytime radio.

The Hummerts were also well rewarded. At a time when the average doctor made less than $5,000 a year and the average lawyer half that, they were each making $100,000 a year from their enterprise, which included several evening musical programs, like "Waltz Time," and mysteries, including the haunting "Mr. Keen, Tracer of Lost Persons."

When television began to displace radio, the couple simply retired and enjoyed a well-traveled life of leisure. After her husband's death, Mrs. Hummert gave up their Park Avenue triplex and cut down a bit on her travels, but she continued her active life, which until a few months ago included daily three-mile walks.

Mrs. Hummert, whose son died several years ago, is survived by two granddaughters, Pamela Pigoni of Hinckley, Ill., and Anne Jeskey of Park Ridge, Ill., and two great-grandchildren.

July 21, 1996

MILTON RUBINCAM,
TOP GENEALOGIST, DIES AT 88

Milton Rubincam, a dogged and inspired researcher who spent the better part of his life swinging through family trees, sometimes finding plums, sometimes snapping off favorite branches, died on Tuesday at a hospital in Washington.

Mr. Rubincam, who lived in Hyattsville, Md., was 88 and known as the dean of American genealogists.

Although he had a respectable career in Government, working in a succession of Federal posts from 1939 until his retirement in 1972 as chief of security for the foreign operations office at the Commerce Department, it was on nights and weekends that Mr. Rubincam came alive.

It was then that the real Rubincam emerged, a man so obsessed with the quest for ancestral authenticity that he haunted libraries and courthouse basements, poring over marriage, birth, death, land, probate and other records, then spending hours typing up his voluminous notes.

Long before he became a full-time genealogist in 1972, pursuing his own research and working for private clients, Mr. Rubincam, a largely self-taught man who attended Temple University and American University but never graduated, had established himself as a genealogical authority.

In the 1960's, for example, he was the president of the exclusive American Society of Genealogists, limited to 50 members. Along the way he became a landmark at the National Genealogical Society, serving four two-year terms as its president in the 1940's and 50's, editing the society's quarterly journal, spending 25 years as its book review editor and turning out 2,000 reviews of his own.

A protégé of Donald Lines Jacobus, the father of modern American scientific genealogy—in which a requirement for firm documentary evidence replaced vague and sometimes fanciful family recollections as the basis for genealogical research—Mr. Rubincam was a master at ferreting out the obscure official document or assembling the mass of subsidiary evidence that would establish a crucial family link.

Sometimes, to be sure, the evidence would not be there, or would point in the wrong direction.

As a result, more than a few of Mr. Rubincam's clients were dismayed to learn that they were not in fact descended from the luminaries whose presumed connection to their families had prompted them to engage him in the first place.

He learned early not to trust everything he saw in print, especially if it appeared in one of the wave of family genealogies produced in the late 19th century after President Ulysses S. Grant, to help commemorate the national centennial in 1876, urged all Americans to record their family histories for posterity.

Milton Rubincam was born in Philadelphia and grew up in Ocean City, N.J., where his widowed mother ran a hotel. He traced his interest in genealogy to childhood tales told by his Uncle Al about the illustrious Rubincam family and its descent from Charlemagne. The name Rubincam was French, his uncle said, and meant "field of blood."

As he never tired of recounting, it was not until Mr. Rubincam, fired by his uncle's stories, began digging into his ancestry that he learned the name was German and meant something like "field of turnips," a discovery that prompted a friend to draw up a Rubincam family crest dominated by a turnip rampant.

By the time he uncovered the awful truth about the Rubincams (their earliest known progenitors were Protestant preachers, not potentates) it was too late: Mr. Rubincam was hooked on genealogy.

But then he was a man who was uncommonly loyal to his childhood passions. When he was 12 he met an Ocean City girl named Priscilla Teasdale and never looked back. They were married in 1935 and remained together until his death.

For all his devotion to his wife, she and her family were victims of one of Mr. Rubincam's most devastating research projects. After tracing his own family back to 16th-century Germany (and producing a book on the Philadelphia Rittenhouses from whom he was also descended), he turned his attention to his wife's family—and proceeded to prove that they were not descended from the signer of the Declaration of Independence they had long regarded as an ancestor.

Not to worry. As consolation, Mr. Rubincam offered incontrovertible proof that his wife was a descendant of a noted Revolutionary War general—through an illegitimate child he fathered in an illicit union with the nurse of his legitimate daughter.

In addition to his wife, Mr. Rubincam is survived by three sons, John, of Hyattsville, Milton 3d, of Rockville, Md., and David, of Lanham, Md., and one grandson—none of whom have shown any inclination to follow in Mr. Rubincam's genealogical footsteps.

As his son John said, "We were victims of genealogical overkill."

September 14, 1997

Mason Rankin, 56, Is Dead;

Founded AIDS Group in Utah

Mason Rankin, a Salt Lake City businessman who had such an abundance of compassion for people with AIDS that he kept scores of volunteer knitters furiously clicking away to supply afghans, sweaters, scarves and hats to people in Utah's H.I.V. community, died on Sept. 21 at a hospital in Salt Lake City. He was 56.

Friends said the cause was chronic obstructive pulmonary disease, a lung disorder.

Mr. Rankin, a lifelong Salt Lake City resident, passed up college to help support his divorced mother and became a successful real estate broker and promoter. He was a hard-driving, hard-drinking businessman whose ventures included assembling the real estate parcel for the Salt Palace convention center.

But for all his business success, it was not until after he had stopped drinking, developed AIDS and been forced to give up his profession that Mr. Rankin discovered his true mission in life: making people with AIDS—and those who helped them—feel good about themselves through the unlikely medium of knitted yarn.

Kindly Gifts, the decidedly offbeat charity Mr. Rankin founded eight years ago, would seem a curious way to help people with AIDS and H.I.V.: Even though many AIDS patients develop circulation problems, making them susceptible to chills, warm clothing is not in short supply in Utah. However, providing protection against the cold was never the point of Kindly Gifts, as became apparent when those who received Mr. Rankin's offerings responded with effusive expressions of gratitude far out of proportion to the utilitarian value of the scarves or hats they had received.

As Mr. Rankin saw it, the recipients recognized what had been obvious to him from the beginning, that the handmade woolens turned out by a growing corps of dedicated volunteers had been touched by love.

And so, as his friends came to see it, had everyone who came in contact with Mr. Rankin, a man of such enthusiasm that once his charity got rolling, it attracted a widening circle of unlikely volunteer knitters, from harried young Mormon mothers to business and professional people, some so determined to take part that they had to be taught to knit.

Mr. Rankin had learned the rudiments of knitting from his mother, but his early efforts were limited to cotton dishcloths until friends who received them as gifts taught him more elaborate techniques.

Kindly Gifts originated when Mr. Rankin and a few friends gathered at his apartment for evenings that were like modern-day quilting bees.

Initially, to pay for the yarn, the group sold the items, giving the profits to various AIDS charities, but once word of their enterprise got around, selling proved unnecessary. Kindly Gifts was inundated with so many gifts of cash and donated yarn that Mr. Rankin's spare bedroom came to resemble a warehouse.

Although a core group continued to gather at his apartment for weekly knitting sessions, the effort attracted many other knitters who worked at home.

To some of his friends, one of the more appealing benefits of the charity was that it attracted a number of elderly volunteers for whom the familiar act of knitting or crocheting became a way to relate to a baffling world beyond their experience.

When one of the most dedicated volunteers, a woman in her 90's, was asked by a puzzled friend why she was working for people with AIDS, she had a ready reply: "Because they need me. AIDS is a disease, just like polio, that happened to come along."

Partly because of such attitudes, the charity has grown to 135 volunteers. Members of the group said that last year they turned out 200 afghans, 100 sweaters and hundreds of smaller items—

enough to meet the needs of Utahans with AIDS or H.I.V. as well as to begin assisting young cancer patients at Ronald McDonald House and those with other diseases.

Although some of its knitted goods are sent outside the state, the bulk of Kindly Gifts' donations are distributed within Utah, many of them around Christmas, which may help explain why Mr. Rankin, who began growing a beard this year, took to calling himself Santa Claus.

Mr. Rankin leaves no immediate relatives, but his friends said Kindly Gifts would continue for the same reason Mr. Rankin started it—because, as he put it, "it gives people the warm fuzzies."

September 29, 1997

John Fulton Is Dead at 65;
Spain's First U.S. Matador

John Fulton, a Philadelphia-born artist who worked with cape and sword in the bullrings of Spain, then celebrated his momentary masterpieces of ritual death by painting pictures of the very bulls he had slain using their own blood, died on Friday in a hospital near his home in Seville. He was 65, and had been the first American to qualify as a matador in Spain.

Friends said the cause was a heart attack.

In more than 40 years as a professional bullfighter, Mr. Fulton was never more than a competent journeyman. But he had his moments, winning grudging respect in Spain and becoming a cult hero to a coterie of American fans.

As an American, and one too poor to bribe his way into the tight circle of sometimes corrupt breeders and promoters who controlled Spanish bullfighting, Mr. Fulton was more than an anomaly.

A few other Americans, including the Brooklyn-born Sydney Franklin, had fought bulls in Spain as early as the 1930's, but Mr. Fulton was the first to be elevated and confirmed as a matador in Spain. He had to endure years of fighting lesser bulls, though, often without pay, in remote arenas before he became a full matador in 1963, a decade after he had killed his first bull in Mexico.

Even then he had trouble getting fights with good bulls in top arenas. He apparently never thought of giving up, but then Mr. Fulton was first and last an artist—and to him bullfighting was pure art.

"It is the most difficult art form in the world," he once said. "You are required to create a work of art spontaneously with a semi-unknown medium, which can kill you, in front of one of the most critical audiences around. And it all leaves only a memory."

But, he said, it involves an exquisite exhilaration that peaks at the moment the sword is plunged into the bull's heart but that lingers long after the climactic kill: "The skies look bluer, the birds sound better, the food tastes better, the wine is better, friendships deepen."

Mr. Fulton pursued his obsession with such single-minded determination it is tempting to wonder what might have become of him if as a child living in a Philadelphia row house he had not seen "Blood and Sand," the movie starring Rita Hayworth and Tyrone Power as a doomed bullfighter.

He was 12 when he saw it, the son of a Hungarian-born mother and an Italian housepainter who changed his name from Schoccitti to Short. (Mr. Fulton, whose given name was Fulton John, dropped the Short when he discovered Spaniards could not pronounce it and reversed his first and middle names.)

The movie so stirred his sense of gallantry and romance that he decided on the spot to become a bullfighter. If a Rita Hayworth was the reward, he told friends years later, it was worth the effort and the risk.

(Robert Daley)

In keeping with matador tradition, Mr. Fulton did have his share of romantic conquests. But he never married, apparently in deference to the Spanish-born high school sweetheart who broke his heart—but not his spirit— by marrying someone else.

By then Mr. Fulton had learned flamenco dancing, and, under the supervision of a bullfighting barber he met through his dance teacher, made his first mock passes using a barber's apron as a cape.

After a year at the Philadelphia Museum College of Art, Mr. Fulton obtained a scholarship to an art school in San Miguel de Allende, which was also a Mexican bullfighting center, and used it to learn bullfighting.

During a two-year Army stint in San Antonio, he spent weekends fighting bulls in Mexican border towns. Then in 1956 he headed for Spain.

For all the obstacles he faced there, Mr. Fulton received his share of encouragement. Ernest Hemingway once slipped him a $100 traveler's check, and James A. Michener was so impressed he used Mr. Fulton as a guide while researching his 1968 book, "Iberia," then devoted much of the book to Mr. Fulton.

He made so little from bullfighting he had to supplement his income. He sold art, including his blood paintings of bulls, served as the actor Peter O'Toole's double during the filming of "Lawrence of Arabia," wrote a book, "Bullfighting" (Dial), and, more recently, worked as a sort of celebrity bullfighting guide for package tours.

Although he could hardly make ends meet, Mr. Fulton became famous for his generosity and his hospitality. His large house in Seville became a social center and crash pad for aspiring matadors he tutored without pay, and he once became so distraught at the sight of a gypsy youngster living in squalor that he adopted the boy.

When Mr. Fulton returned to San Miguel in 1994 for his last kill at the age of 61, it was his son, Federico, who snipped off his father's ponytail, a traditional ritual for a matador's retirement.

Since then, Mr. Fulton had been working on his autobiography, a work the man who spent his life tilting at cultural windmills planned to call, "The Memoirs of John Quixote."

February 23, 1998

41

Virginia Mae Morrow Dies at 70;
Created Bridey Murphy Hoopla

Virginia Mae Morrow, the Colorado woman whose hypnosis-induced recollections created a sensation in the 1950's, died on July 12 at a hospice outside Denver. She was 70.

The cause was cancer, her husband, Richard, said.

According to Mrs. Morrow's own recollections, she had died before, after falling down a flight of stairs in Ireland in 1864, when she was known as Bridey Murphy.

Whether Mrs. Morrow really had a past life as Bridey Murphy, or even if there was a Bridey Murphy who lived the life Mrs. Morrow so vividly described in a thick Irish brogue during taped hypnotic sessions in 1952 and 1953, has been the subject of intense emotional debate for more than four decades.

The debate began when her story was first told in articles by William J. Barker in The Denver Post in 1954, and it engaged a far wider audience when "The Search for Bridey Murphy" was published by Doubleday in 1956 and made into a movie the same year.

The book was by Morey Bernstein, the amateur hypnotist who had elicited the recollections in Pueblo, Colo. It became a best seller and was reissued in 1965 with additional material by Mr. Barker, but has been out of print for several years.

Whether Mrs. Morrow's account was dismissed out of hand or accepted as proof of reincarnation, Bridey Murphy became a 1950's phenomenon rivaling the Hula-Hoop. There were Bridey Murphy parties ("come as you were") and Bridey Murphy jokes (parents greeting newborns with "Welcome back").

The book triggered an interest in reincarnation and the use of hypnosis to regress a subject to early childhood, and perhaps beyond. It also spawned efforts to debunk Mrs. Morrow's recollections.

The notion that the book was an out-and-out hoax never gained much credence for several reasons. Mr. Bernstein, for example, was a wealthy and highly respected Pueblo businessman who had been experimenting with hypnosis for years.

His hypnosis sessions with Mrs. Morrow, which began on a lark after a party, were conducted in front of respected witnesses who vouched for the apparent authenticity of Mrs. Morrow's regression.

Also, Mrs. Morrow, then a 27-year-old mother of two known as Ginny Tighe, seemed an entirely guileless subject. She insisted that her real name not be used in the book, which called her Ruth Simmons, and then shunned virtually every opportunity to cash in on the Bridey Murphy phenomenon.

Efforts to debunk Bridey Murphy focused on the assumption that her detailed recollections of an Irish life a century earlier were simply an outpouring of long-forgotten childhood memories.

In the 1965 edition, Mr. Barker took on the debunkers point by point. Yes, for example, as a child in Chicago Mrs. Morrow had lived across the street from a woman named Bridey (a common diminutive of Bridget), but so what? Mrs. Morrow said she had never known the woman's first name.

As for the visiting aunt of Scotch-Irish extraction who supposedly regaled her with tales from Ireland, the woman was born in New York and had no special interest in Ireland, and Mrs. Morrow was 18, not an impressionable toddler, when she was around.

Mrs. Morrow, whose original name was Reese, was born in Madison, Wis., on April 27, 1925, and raised by an aunt and uncle in Chicago. After studying at Northwestern University, she went with a friend to Denver, where she got a job and met her first husband, Hugh Tighe, who was later transferred to Pueblo.

They later moved back to the Denver area and were divorced.

Whatever the explanation of her highly detailed recollections, the one person who seemed immune to the debate was Mrs. Morrow.

As for all the fuss she had kicked up, she once said, "If I had known what was going to happen I would never have lain down on the couch."

In addition to her husband, of Englewood, Colo., Mrs. Morrow is survived by the three children from her first marriage, Marilou Butler of Valdosta, Ga., Nanci Lee of Hong Kong and Teri Francis of San Jose, Calif.; two stepchildren, Pam Zimmer of El Cajon, Calif., and Randy Morrow of Littleton, Colo., and 10 grandchildren.

July 21, 1995

Hal Lipset,

Private Detective with a Difference,

Dies at 78

Hal Lipset, a storied San Francisco sleuth who helped elevate, or rather reduce, electronic surveillance to a miniature art, died on Monday at a San Francisco hospital. He was 78 and was best known as the man who put a bug in a martini olive.

Friends said the cause was heart failure during treatment for an aneurysm.

Despite a half century in which he regularly broke into hotel rooms to catch errant spouses and cheerfully represented the most disreputable clients, Mr. Lipset was widely credited with transforming the once seedy gumshoe calling into a respected profession.

But then Mr. Lipset was a detective with a difference, a private eye who shunned the hard-boiled Sam Spade image, except for occasional effect, and took as his fictional role model Perry Mason's right-hand man, Paul Drake.

At a time when private detectives were regarded as little more than lawyers' errand boys, Mr. Lipset was soon working in virtual partnership with San Francisco's leading lawyers.

Along the way he became a San Francisco legend, partly because he ran his business from his 25-room mansion in Pacific Heights and partly because he was a mainstay in Herb Caen's column in The San Francisco Chronicle, a position he cemented when he chased a pair of jewel thieves across Europe, sending daily dispatches on his progress to Mr. Caen and a breathless San Francisco until he caught up with them in the Canary Islands.

Mr. Lipset, who trained many detectives who eventually set up their own agencies, was known for recruiting intellectual operatives, among them a former philosophy professor and Patricia Holt, now The Chronicle's book editor, who wrote his 1995 biography, "The Bug in the Martini Olive."

A native of Newark who briefly attended the University of California at Berkeley, Mr. Lipset received his training as an Army investigator in Europe in World War II, then settled in San Francisco, where he and his wife, Lynn, opened an agency in 1947.

Mr. Lipset used a wire recorder from the beginning, but it was the introduction of transistors in the 1950's that gave him the vision that would make him famous.

Working closely with an electronics expert, Ralph Bersche, Mr. Lipset let his imagination run wild, once winning over a skeptical prospective client by playing a recording of a conversation they had had while sitting naked in a steam room. (The suspicious client had neglected to inspect his bar of soap.)

For all such eye-catching applications. Mr. Lipset did much of his best work fully dressed using a holstered recorder to pick up damaging statements made by a rival witness. When the witness would lie in court about the conversation, and lawyers would challenge Mr. Lipset's veracity, the recording would establish the truth.

Aware of widespread invasions of privacy by law enforcement and others, he campaigned for reasonable restrictions and worked closely with Sam Dash, a former Philadelphia prosecutor, on his 1959 book, "The Eavesdroppers."

The book laid the groundwork for reform, but Mr. Dash said that it was Mr. Lipset's riveting demonstration of a bugged martini glass before a Senate subcommittee in 1968 that focused public opinion on the issue.

Never mind that the tiny transmitter inside a fake olive with a microphone instead of pimento and a toothpick as an antenna had a severely limited range, that it would not work at all if there were actual gin and vermouth in the glass and that it was built purely for show.

The olive became the symbol of how easy transmitters were to conceal. A 1968 Federal law banned all wiretapping and recordings without a court order unless at least one party to the conversation had consented. But much to Mr. Dash's horror, and Mr. Lipset's chagrin, California, and later other states, banned private recordings unless all participants consent.

As the Senate Watergate Committee's counsel, Mr. Dash hired Mr. Lipset as chief investigator in 1973, but when the Nixon White House leaked the fact that Mr. Lipset had been convicted of a minor eavesdropping offense, Mr. Dash, who had been aware of the incident, let him resign.

Mr. Dash, who was once accused of using Mr. Lipset to offer a $10,000 bribe to a union dissident who had offered information while Mr. Dash was representing a Philadelphia teamsters' union local, still shudders at what might have happened if the police had searched the detective.

The secret recording Mr. Lipset made of his conversation with the dissident put the lie to the charge.

Mr. Lipset, whose wife died in 1964, is survived by two sons, Louis of San Francisco and Lawrence of Mendocino, Calif., and one grandchild.

December 12, 1997

R. V. PATWARDHAN,

HINDU PRIEST WITH NEW YORK VERVE,

DIES AT 79

Ramachandra V. Patwardhan, who long provided the cultural and religious thread that knitted New York's Indian community together as the city's only Hindu priest, died on May 30 at St. Vincent's Hospital in Greenwich Village. He was 79.

His wife, Tara, said the cause was congestive heart failure.

For the better part of three decades, Mr. Patwardhan was an indispensable figure in New York's Hindu community, the man in the dhoti and turban who by virtue of his priestly birth and his religious training could do what no other Hindu in New York could do, officiate at the elaborate wedding and other ceremonies that have been the hallmark of Hinduism for 2,500 years.

It may seem surprising now, but despite the city's reputation as a melting pot, the entire Indian presence in New York consisted of just a handful of journalists, diplomats and students on temporary visas when Mr. Patwardhan arrived from India in 1947 to study international law at New York University. The race-based immigration laws of the era simply precluded significant migration from the Asian subcontinent.

Mr. Patwardhan, himself a native of Pandharpur who had studied law and practiced with his father, had fully expected to return to India, but in the aftermath of the country's independence from Britain in 1947, he accepted a job at the Indian consulate, summoned his wife, who also worked at the consulate, and took an apartment on Perry Street that became his home for almost 50 years.

Mr. Patwardhan, who explored his adopted city during daily five-mile walks, quickly realized there were drawbacks to being a member of a tiny minority in an alien culture, among them the inability to practice his religion in a city where the few Hindu residents included no priests.

As a Brahmin, or member of the priestly caste, and one who had also mastered Sanskrit and Hinduism's Vedic texts, Mr. Patwardhan needed no other qualifications to become a priest, so he decided to fill the void.

The first wedding ceremony he performed, in 1956, was considered such an exotic novelty that it was broadcast live on television. Indeed, a Hindu priest was such a rarity in the United States that Mr. Patwardhan was soon traveling all over the country to perform weddings.

For a while there were so few Hindus in New York that he performed only the occasional wedding, but after the immigration laws were liberalized in the 1960's, touching off a flood of migration from India, Mr. Patwardhan was in such demand that he quit his job in 1968.

In time, the wave of immigration brought other Hindu priests to the city, but Mr. Patwardhan remained a favorite, partly because the man known as Nana, Panditji or simply Pat had become a venerated figure and partly because he had virtually patented the New York–style Hindu wedding ceremony.

In India, weddings sometimes last for days, but Mr. Patwardhan, mindful of the peculiar pace of life in New York, streamlined the ceremony, distilling it to its essence, and in an innovation that would have shocked the sometimes austere and rigid priests in India, he interlaced the service with English explanations that kept the children in attendance enthralled and provided many young Hindu-Americans with their only training in their ancestral religion.

Mr. Patwardhan sometimes had to provide similar instruction to the elders. After a couple had set a date, it was not uncommon for a grandmother, armed with astrological tables, to protest that the time was not auspicious. Mr. Patwardhan would gently explain that the eternal truths of the Veda were stronger than superstition and most certainly did not depend on the coincidental alignment of the stars, and then the wedding would proceed on schedule.

Perhaps his most inspired New York innovation concerned the heart of the Hindu wedding ceremony, fire, the sacred witness to whom the priestly hymns and chants and the couple's vows are addressed. In India the intricate arrangement of mighty logs precisely specified by the Veda can sometimes produce quite a conflagration, so the ceremonies are often performed outdoors.

Mr. Patwardhan, who performed most of his ceremonies in small apartments and was as respectful of the city's fire laws as he was disdainful of superstition, simply created a symbolic wedding fire by arranging tiny strips of wood in a small brazier and setting them alight.

His wife is his only survivor.

June 23, 1996

Sidney Grossman, 91;

Entrepreneur Headed

Lumber Concern

Sidney Grossman, an innovative entrepreneur who salvaged forests, sold Army tanks for tractors, turned home buyers into home builders and recycled entire towns, died on Thursday at his home in West Newton, Mass. He was 91 and had been president of his family's lumber business in Quincy, Mass., from 1948 to 1968.

To say that Mr. Grossman thought big would be an understatement. Perhaps because he was the adored baby in a family of nine children, Mr. Grossman grew up to become a distinctly gregarious man, one whose magnetic personality made him a master salesman even as his lifelong penchant for dreaming earned him a reputation for the grand conceptualization.

By the time he joined his father and older brothers in the family business, L. Grossman & Sons, straight out of high school in the early 1920's, the business had changed considerably since 1881, when his father, Louis Grossman, arrived from Russia and began selling needles and other notions door to door from a backpack.

As the founder's grandson, David Grossman, was telling it yesterday, the critical juncture came in 1900 after Mr. Grossman had moved up to a horse and wagon and began delivering animal bones to a factory outside Quincy for processing into roofing shingles.

He was starting back after making a delivery when a factory executive, chiding him for missing an opportunity, provided what became a family rallying cry: "Grossman, don't go home empty."

Accepting the challenge, Mr. Grossman loaded his wagon with shingles, found a ready market in Quincy, eventually added lumber and other building materials to his line and laid the groundwork for what became the largest lumber and home-supply retailing operation in the region. When it was sold in 1969, it had stores in seven states from Maine to New York.

No one ever needed to remind Sidney Grossman not to go home empty. By the time he took charge of the company in 1948 he had already established his reputation for turning disaster into profit.

His first major coup came in the wake of the 1938 hurricane that devastated New England, killing hundreds of people and felling millions of trees. After the Federal Government paid owners for the damaged trees, Mr. Grossman persuaded the family to buy the trees from the Government and to set up a network of sawmills to process them into lumber.

It was a daring move in 1938, but paid off. The multimillion-dollar deal produced 800 million board feet of lumber.

Mr. Grossman, who enlisted in the Army Reserve in 1934 and was called to active duty in the summer of 1941, developed his salvage skills further when he was put in charge of salvage operations in France six days after the Normandy invasion. The effort earned him the Army Legion of Merit and provided valuable experience.

Recognizing the profit potential in the vast amounts of war surplus being sold for a pittance, Mr. Grossman again proved his shrewdness, selling rocket tubes for water pipes, for example, and, in his most daring and conspicuous undertaking, selling tanks to farmers for conversion into tractors.

Mr. Grossman, who also knew the value of publicity, kept one parked in front of his Quincy headquarters.

Like William Levitt and others, Mr. Grossman also saw the potential for profit in satisfying the long pent-up demand for homes in the lush years after the war. But unlike Mr. Levitt, who hired armies of construction workers to turn potato fields into vast subdivisions, Mr. Grossman eliminated the labor costs by selling kits, complete with architectural drawings, lumber and other materials, to buyers with a modicum of carpentry skills who could build their homes with the help of friends or relatives.

Thousands of such homes sprang up on vacant lots all over New England, said Mr. Grossman's son, David, who noted that the various models named for his sisters were not hard to spot amid the Cape Cods and other New England housing.

"They look pretty Spartan," he said.

What was surely Mr. Grossman's grandest scheme came when he began recycling entire towns abandoned by textile mills and other employers.

His most notable success was the rescue of Sanford, Me., after Burlington Industries bought and closed the once thriving Goodall Sanford Mills in 1954, transferring the operations to the South and throwing 3,500 of the town's 15,000 residents out of work.

As he did with other one-company towns, Mr. Grossman bought the abandoned factories and other Goodall property, including a country club, an airport and various water rights, and lured a variety of smaller industries to move in, often arranging the financing.

Today Sanford, which became known as "the town that refused to die," is a thriving community of 23,000 people and an array of diversified industries, none employing more than a few hundred people.

In addition to his son, of Newton, Mass., Mr. Grossman is survived by two daughters, Ina Perlmutter of Evanston, Ill., and Beth Blankstein of Waban, Mass.; three sisters, Abba Fleishman and Etta Milchen of Quincy and Sarah Hellmann of Chestnut Hill, Mass.; 13 grandchildren and 12 great-grandchildren.

December 11, 1996

Curtis L. Carlson, 84,

Founder of

Trading Stamp Conglomerate

Curtis L. Carlson, who borrowed $55 from his landlord in 1938 and didn't look back until he had turned a fledgling grocery store trading stamp company into one of the world's largest private businesses, died on Friday at a hospital near his home in Minneapolis. He was 84 and had been the sole owner of the Carlson Companies, an international conglomerate with 150,000 employees and $20 billion in annual revenue.

For a corporation whose more than 100 separate companies include the Radisson and Regent International hotel chains, T.G.I. Friday's and half a dozen other restaurant chains, several travel agencies, a cruise line, the nation's largest marketing services company, vast real estate holdings and a host of other operations in 140 countries, the Carlson Companies had distinctly humble beginnings. So did Mr. Carlson.

Mr. Carlson, the son of a Swedish immigrant who became a neighborhood grocer, had a childhood worthy of a Norman Rockwell painting with highlights by John D. Rockefeller.

He was a golf caddy at 9, had his first newspaper route at 11 and quickly added two others. He also operated a newsstand at a busy intersection, worked his way through college driving a soft-drink truck and engaged in a little light loan-sharking.

In an exercise worthy of selling refrigerators to Eskimos, Mr. Carlson as an 18-year-old summertime bank messenger would lend cash-strapped tellers $5 on a Friday and collect $6 on payday the following Monday, transactions whose three-day interest works out to an annual percentage rate exceeding 2,400 percent.

Somewhat redundantly studying economics at the University of Minnesota, Mr. Carlson graduated in 1937 and went to work as a $110-a-month soap salesman for Procter & Gamble. But he did not stay there for long.

At a time when some local department stores were seeking to assure repeat business by giving customers Security Red trading stamps, exchangeable for premiums, Mr. Carlson realized that such stamps would be ideal for grocery stores, whose identical products left them little room to distinguish themselves from the pack.

Acting on his vision, Mr. Carlson created the Gold Bond Stamp Company in 1938, with a $55 loan—and a bit of skulduggery: He paid a department store secretary $10 for a copy of the Security Red Stamp master contract, which became his blueprint.

The idea was that a grocer would pay Mr. Carlson $14.50 for stamps that could be exchanged for products that cost $10 whole-sale but had a much higher retail value. That made the stamps attractive to the grocer and to the store's customers, but not at first glance to Mr. Carlson, whose $4.50 spread would barely cover costs and overhead.

The magic of the business was that while the grocer would pay for the stamps as they were issued, it might be months before customers accumulated enough stamps to redeem them (a four-slice toaster proved to be the most popular premium) and some would not be redeemed at all, leaving Mr. Carlson with the float—the use of the money—for other investments.

The trick was to sell the program to enough stores to create a sizable float. But as a salesman, Mr. Carlson—who married his college sweetheart, Arlene Martin, about the time he started the business—was shameless. To draw attention to his program he had his wife dress up in an eye-catching drum majorette uniform and march through prospective stores extolling the glories of Gold Bond stamps.

By 1941, he had signed up 200 accounts, but shortages cre-ated by World War II made sales incentives superfluous, and for a while he had to take a job with his father-in-law's clothing business.

Once the war was over in 1945, expansion came steadily. Indeed, Gold Bond did well enough to finance a series of important acquisitions. By 1962, the company had major investments in suburban Minneapolis real estate, including the site of what became its $300 million headquarters in Minnetonka, and acquired the downtown Radisson Hotel, which rapidly expanded into a 350-hotel chain.

As a result of the diversification, when the stamp business began to decline in 1968, the company continued to thrive. It changed its name to the Carlson Companies in 1973.

According to company figures, annual revenue, which did not reach $1 million until 1952, had climbed to $100 million by 1968, reached $1 billion in 1976 and topped $10 billion in 1993, with most of the growth resulting from a blistering pace of diversification.

Although he acquired an 85-foot yacht, a luxurious hunting lodge, a family compound at Lake Minnetonka and other trappings of wealth, Mr. Carlson found nothing quite so much fun as business.

Accordingly, he became known as such a hands-on boss that his executives made few major decisions, though they rarely complained. He paid them so well (the top 25 getting new luxury cars every year) that they were said to be bound to the company by golden handcuffs.

Never tempted to sell stock to the public, Mr. Carlson took pains a decade ago to keep his company private—and in family hands—after his death by placing all his businesses in a holding company, which his two daughters, Marilyn Nelson and Barbara Gage, will now jointly own. He also set up trusts to hold nonvoting stock for his eight grandchildren, six great-grandchildren and other relatives.

Mr. Carlson, who is also survived by his wife, Arlene, and by a brother, Warren, was so devoted to his business that after a brief retirement and quadruple bypass heart surgery, he resumed control in 1991 and continued to run the business until retiring again last year in favor of his elder daughter, Marilyn.

A man who gave millions to the University of Minnesota and other charities, Mr. Carlson insisted the lure of money was not what drove him. "You keep score with the money you make," he once said, "but you've got to get a thrill out of doing something that works."

February 22, 1999

Minnesota Fats,

a Real Hustler with a Pool Cue,

Is Dead

Rudolf Walter Wanderone, the charming, slick-talking pool hustler who labored largely in obscurity until he reinvented himself in the 1960's by claiming to be Minnesota Fats, died yesterday at his home in Nashville. He was 82, or perhaps 95.

With Fats, who insisted he was the prototype of the fictional character portrayed by Jackie Gleason in the movie "The Hustler," the only certainty was that you could never know for sure.

His wife, Theresa, said the cause of death was congestive heart failure.

Both she and his first wife, Evaline, insisted that he would have been 83 today although Fats, who long claimed to have been born in 1900, had taken to calling the 1913 birth date that appeared in a 1966 biography his "baseball age."

In a career in which he may or may not have sailed around the world six times, survived two shipwrecks and hobnobbed, as he claimed, with the likes of Clark Gable, Arnold Rothstein, Damon Runyon and Al Capone, his age was as slippery as his moves around a pool table.

Although he had in fact made his living since the 1920's criss-crossing the country taking on all comers, until "The Hustler" came out in 1961, nobody beyond the small coterie of pool hustlers and their eager marks had heard of him.

But Mr. Wanderone, a New York native whose various nicknames had in fact included New York Fats, knew an opportunity when he saw one. He simply adopted the name Minnesota Fats, claiming that the character portrayed by Gleason in the 1961 movie had been based on his life.

Walter Tevis, the author of the original novel, consistently denied the claim, but it was a measure of Mr. Wanderone's mesmerizing ways that his widow insisted yesterday that before the author's death Mr. Tevis had made a hefty settlement to her husband to avoid a lawsuit, a claim the former Mrs. Wanderone scoffed at.

"Fats never got a quarter," she said.

It was an index of Mr. Wanderone's grasp of human psychology and his own impish appeal that he realized that it didn't make any difference whether he had been Minnesota Fats before the 1960's.

Within months after he decided to cash in on his borrowed fame, Mr. Wanderone, or Minnesota Fats, was a celebrity, appearing on television, making nationwide tours and passing out stamped autograph cards proclaiming himself the greatest pool player ever.

(AP/Wide World Photos)

He certainly looked like a Minnesota Fats, or at least some Fats. At 5 feet 10 inches, Mr. Wanderone had weighed as much as 300 pounds.

Mr. Wanderone, who did not drink but was famous for his love of ice cream, pies or anything sweet, never apologized for his appetite.

As he told it in his 1966 biography, "The Bank Shot and Other Great Robberies," by Tom Fox, "I've been eating like a sultan since I was 2 days old. I had a mother and three sisters who worshiped me, and when I was 2 years old they used to plop me in a bed with a jillion satin pillows and spray me with exotic perfumes and lilac water and then they would shoot me the grapes."

The early pampering perhaps explains why Mr. Wanderone, who once said he never picked up anything heavier than a silver dollar, grew up with a fierce aversion to physical labor, so much so that on their cross-country trips his wife was expected to do all the driving, carry all the luggage and even change the flat tires.

"Change a tire?" Mr. Wanderone once exclaimed. "I'd rather change cars."

Although his frequent claim that he had never lost a game "when the cheese was on the table," was more fabrication than exaggeration, according to his first wife, Mr. Wanderone was in fact a master hustler who tended to be just as good as he needed to be when he needed to be.

"He knew how to manage money," she said, insisting that while the late Willie Mosconi, the perennial professional champion, may have been correct in claiming to have won the vast majority of their games, "Fats always left with the money."

During their years together, she said, "We lived like kings."

Mr. Wanderone, who had a weakness for Cadillacs and other expensive cars, was also known as an easy touch, one who never said no to a loan and who was so fond of animals he adopted dozens of them.

He also had an acknowledged weakness for women, or "the tomatoes," as he called them.

According to both of his wives, Mr. Wanderone was a courtly man of the old school, one who, for example, would inevitably remind his opponents to watch their language whenever he would escort his first wife into some dingy pool hall.

He also knew how to take care of himself, the first Mrs. Wanderone said, recalling how she would sometimes be waiting in a convertible outside a backstreet pool room when her husband, having cleaned out the customers inside, would be forced to fight his way out.

"In his hands a pool cue was as good a weapon as a knife," she said.

Mr. Wanderone, whose father was a seagoing Swiss immigrant, was born in the Washington Heights section of Manhattan on Jan. 19, apparently in 1913 (although he once claimed to have been hustling as early as 1910).

He traced his interest in the sport to an uncle who used to take him to saloons and plop him down on the pool table when he was 2. "The pool table was my crib," he said.

Dropping out of school in the eighth grade, he accompanied his father to Europe on several trips, once studying with a Swiss pool champion.

However, he learned the game. He learned it well enough to support himself without having to take an actual job, although he would have been far better off, his first wife said, had he been able to stay away from gambling at the dice tables.

Curiously, after he became Minnesota Fats, his new persona led to an actual job, something he had studiously avoided. He went to work for a pool equipment company, spending so much time making personal appearances across the country and coming home so grumpy, his first wife said, that she finally divorced him in 1985.

Mr. Wanderone then settled in Nashville, settling in a subsidized celebrity suite at the Hermitage Hotel, where he spent his days feeding bread crumbs to the pigeons in a nearby park and his evenings stamping autographs in Music City honky-tonks.

Mr. Wanderone, whose nonstop braggadocio banter had made generations of pool hall denizens laugh, was as charming as ever. In 1992, when he expressed fear of being declared incompetent and becoming a ward of the state, he married 27-year-old Theresa Bell. She nursed him around the clock except, she said yesterday, when she would stay at home while her husband and her boyfriend went bar-hopping.

She is his only survivor.

January 19, 1996

J. K. Stout,

Pioneering Judge in Pennsylvania,

Is Dead at 79

Juanita Kidd Stout, an Oklahoma music teacher turned Philadelphia lawyer who became the first black woman to serve as a judge in Pennsylvania, then spent the better part of 40 years as a judicial scourge of murder, mayhem and bad grammar, died on Friday at a hospital near her home in Philadelphia. She was 79 and throughout a long pioneering legal career had been first and foremost an English teacher.

Friends said the cause of death was leukemia.

It may not say much about Pennsylvania that the first black woman to gain a seat on a state bench was born in Wewoka, Okla., received a bachelor's degree from the University of Iowa and studied law at Indiana University, but it is to the state's credit that once Judge Stout established a practice in Philadelphia in 1954 it did not take the local legal community long to recognize that it had gained a treasure.

Within two years she had been appointed to the District Attorney's office, where she promptly extended her reputation as "the hardest working lawyer in Philadelphia." Getting up at 4 A.M. seven days a week to study law, cases and evidence, she became so well known for her preparation, and for her successful prosecutions, that it seemed hardly surprising that she would win swift appointment to the bench.

When she did, in 1959, on an interim appointment to the old Philadelphia Municipal Court, she came up for election two months later and won handily, becoming the first black woman in the country to win election to a court of record.

She was later appointed to the Philadelphia Court of Common Pleas, where she specialized in homicide cases. In 1988, she received an interim appointment to the Pennsylvania Supreme Court, making her the first black woman in the country to be a judge on a state's highest court, a position she held for a year, until she turned 70, the court's mandatory retirement age, and returned to the bench in Philadelphia.

She dealt firmly with offenders and despised crime, but seemed to reserve her greatest fury for what she perceived as its underlying cause, an almost willful ignorance, especially among defendants who had dropped out of school without learning to read and write.

Slackers could expect no leniency, but if she saw a glimmer of remorse and a spark of resolve to do better, Judge Stout, who had a fine eye for the line between teenage excess and hard-core crime, could be accommodating. One gang member who was sentenced to time at reform school rather than at a harsher correctional facility, later became her law clerk and went on to establish a large law firm.

In one of her more celebrated cases, while assigned to juvenile court in 1965, within 24 hours after a white sailor from Georgia was severely beaten while trying to defend a 16-year-old white girl from being raped at a subway station by eight black gang members, Judge Stout had tried, convicted and sentenced seven of the thugs to long prison terms and placed the eighth on probation.

"Rape today, jail tomorrow," she suggested, might be an effective deterrent.

This and several other long sentences she imposed on violent gang members over the next few weeks made Judge Stout such a hero in Philadelphia that when the executive director of the local chapter of the American Civil Liberties Union sent form letters to members of the Philadelphia bar protesting her "swift justice," he received so many angry replies that he sent a second letter, beginning, "I am sorry that our criticism of Judge Stout has upset you."

Her tough stance made her a pariah to local gangs, and when her mail included a number of death threats, Judge Stout was predictably outraged. The grammar was atrocious, she said, and the letters were riddled with misspellings.

Indeed, she gave so many impassioned lectures on the importance of education that youthful defendants learned to assure her that they attended school regularly, a tactic that might have worked more often if Judge Stout had not learned to check school attendance records.

She routinely sentenced first-time offenders to write long essays, and was such a stickler for proper usage that she blithely corrected her fellow judges' grammar, and woe betide the lawyer who sought to "appraise" her of something.

"I know my value," she would snap. "Now if you want to apprise me, get on with it."

When lawyers sought leniency for their youthful clients on the ground that they had deprived upbringings, Judge Stout was unmoved. "We didn't have indoor plumbing until I was 13," she once said, rejecting poverty as an excuse for crime.

She might have grown up poor, but her parents were both teachers, and Judge Stout, who credited her mother with instilling her lifelong habit of hard work, learned to read at 3, entered the third grade at 6 and started college at 16, first at a black school in nearby Missouri and later at the University of Iowa before returning to Oklahoma as a music teacher.

For all her later education, she credited her accidental legal career to a high school shorthand course. Seeking work in Washington in World War II, she landed a job at a law firm and was so good at taking legal dictation that she began to study law, first in Washington and later at Indiana University, where she obtained two law degrees while her husband, Charles Otis Stout, was studying for his doctorate. He died in 1988.

When one of the Washington firm's partners, William H. Hastie, was named to the Court of Appeals in Philadelphia in 1950, he hired his former stenographer as administrative assistant, a position she held until she entered private practice a few years later.

Throughout her career Judge Stout lectured widely, invariably stressing the importance of using correct English, especially when she addressed law students.

In recent years, as she was showered with honors, she modestly suggested they were undeserved but she could hardly complain. The citations hailing her myriad accomplishments were letter-perfect.

August 24, 1998

Sidney Korshak, 88, Dies;

Fabled Fixer for the Chicago Mob

Sidney R. Korshak, a labor lawyer who used his reputation as the Chicago mob's man in Los Angeles to become one of Hollywood's most fabled and influential fixers, died on Saturday at his home in Beverly Hills. He was 88.

His death came a day after that of his brother, Marshall Korshak, a longtime Chicago politician who died in a hospital there at the age of 85.

Although the two brothers shared a law office in Chicago for many years, their careers diverged considerably. Marshall Korshak led a distinctly public life as a glad-handing Democratic machine politician, serving, among other things, as state senator and city treasurer and dispensing thousands of jobs as a ward boss. But Sidney Korshak pursued power in the shadows.

It was a tribute to Sidney Korshak's success that he was never indicted, despite repeated federal and state investigations. And the widespread belief that he had in fact committed the very crimes the authorities could never prove made him an indispensible ally of leading Hollywood producers, corporate executives and politicians.

As his longtime friend and admirer Robert Evans, the former head of Paramount, described it in his 1994 book, "The Kid Stays in the Picture," Mr. Korshak could work wonders with a single phone call, especially when labor problems were an issue.

"Let's just say that a nod from Korshak," Mr. Evans wrote, "and the teamsters change management. A nod from Korshak, and Santa Anita closes. A nod from Korshak, and Vegas shuts down. A nod from Korshak, and the Dodgers can suddenly play night baseball."

Sometimes, to be sure, it took more than one call. At one point when police had him under surveillance, Mr. Korshak, who was careful not to make business calls on telephones that might be tapped, was seen entering a public phone booth carrying a paper bag full of coins.

Although Mr. Korshak generally made his calls to solve major problems faced by clients like the Los Angeles Dodgers, Gulf and Western, M.C.A., Las Vegas hotels and other large corporations, he also used his clout on lesser matters.

Among the stories circulating yesterday, for example, was one about the time the comedian Alan King was turned away at a plush European hotel by a desk clerk who insisted that there were simply no rooms available. Mr. King used a lobby phone to call Mr. Korshak in Los Angeles, and before he hung up, the clerk was knocking at the door of the phone booth to tell Mr. King that his suite was ready.

The son of a wealthy Chicago contractor, Mr. Korshak graduated from the University of Wisconsin and received a law degree from DePaul University in 1930. Within months of opening his law practice, according to extensive research conducted by Seymour M. Hersh and Jeff Gerth for The New York Times in 1976, he was defending members of the Al Capone crime syndicate.

His reputation was made in 1943 when a mobster on trial for extorting millions of dollars from Hollywood movie companies testified that when he had been introduced to Mr. Korshak by a high-ranking Capone mobster, he had been told, "Sidney is our man."

That became even more apparent in 1946, when a Chicago department store chain faced with demands for payoffs from rival unions engaged him, and the problem almost magically disappeared.

Within months, Mr. Korshak, who had been shunned by the city's business elite, was in demand for his services as a labor lawyer who could stave off demands from legitimate unions by arranging instant sweetheart contracts with friendly unions, often the teamsters.

Mr. Korshak, who sometimes boasted that he had paid off judges, solidified his standing among Chicago's business, civic and social leaders by giving ribald late-night parties featuring some of Chicago's most beautiful and willing showgirls.

"Sidney always had contact with high-class girls," a former Chicago judge told The Times in 1976. "Not your $50 girl, but girls costing $250 or more."

Mr. Korshak moved to California in the late 1940's and found Hollywood executives as eager as Chicago businessmen to hire him to insure labor peace.

He added to his reputation and his usefulness when it became known that he could arrange loans of millions of dollars from the teamsters' infamous Central States Pension Fund, which, among other things, helped finance the growth of the Las Vegas casino industry, often with Mr. Korshak serving as the intermediary and sometimes as silent partner.

It was a reflection of his power that when Mr. Korshak showed up unexpectedly at a Las Vegas hotel during a 1961 teamsters' meeting, he was immediately installed in the largest suite, even though the hotel had to dislodge the previous occupant: the union's president, Jimmy Hoffa.

In an era when mob figures were forever being gunned down by rival gangsters or sent to prison by determined prosecutors, Mr. Korshak seemed to lead a charmed life. That was partly because his mansion was protected by extensive security measures, partly because he was adept at using his role as a lawyer as a shield against probing grand jury questions and partly because he was careful to distance himself from the fruits of his own activities.

He never, for example, served as an officer of the various corporations formed to carry out his complex schemes. Even his legal work left no paper trail. Never licensed to practice in California, he maintained no Los Angeles office and had bills mailed from Chicago. He was famous for never taking notes or even reading contracts.

As a result, he became so valuable to the mob and its corrupt union allies that lower-level mobsters were ordered never to approach him, lest they tarnish his reputation for trust and integrity.

At the same time, he was so valuable to more or less legitimate businesses that the executives who hired him would never breathe a word against him.

Mr. Korshak is survived by his wife, Bernice; three children, Harry of London, and Stuart and Katy of Beverly Hills, and five grandchildren.

Marhsall Korshak is survived by his wife, Edith; two daughters, Marjorie Gerson and Hope Rudnick of Chicago; four grandchildren, and four great-grandchildren.

January 22, 1996

Francine Katzenbogen, 51; Gave Cats the Lap of Luxury

Francine Katzenbogen, a Brooklyn-born lottery millionaire who loved cats so much she worked tirelessly for animal adoption agencies, donated generously to their support and housed 20 beloved strays in luxury at her own suburban Los Angeles mansion, died on Oct. 30 at her home in Studio City. She was 51 and may have loved cats rather more than was good for her.

Her aunt, Lorraine Katzenbogen of Spokane, Wash., said the cause was a chronic asthma condition aggravated by strong allergic reactions to the very cats that were her niece's overriding passion.

In 1988, when she won a $7 million jackpot the first time she played the New York State Lottery, Miss Katzenbogen was a cosmetics consultant living at home with her parents and younger brother in Canarsie, where the whole family collected and sheltered stray cats.

Four years later, when a grief-stricken Miss Katzenbogen decided to move to the West Coast after the deaths of her mother and brother, she never considered leaving the cats behind, or allowing them to travel without her. So she booked space for herself and her brood on a cargo plane, packed up cats, Katzenbogen, kit and caboodle and, at a cost of some $8,000, including $4,000 in mandatory veterinary fees, flew off to a new life in Los Angeles. Her father, Irving, a retired housepainter, later joined her.

Even before she arrived and settled into a $1 million Studio City estate she had bought three years earlier, Miss Katzenbogen, who had deferred an earlier planned move after her mother became ill, found that she was not entirely welcome in her exclusive new neighborhood.

Her neighbors were not amused that she planned to house 20 cats in a converted two-story garage she had refurbished at a cost of $100,000. The luxurious cat complex included tile floors, climbing towers, scratching posts, skylights and cozy, low-lying window ledges where the cats could stretch out and watch the world outside their air-conditioned lair.

In Brooklyn, where a fictional cat named Rhubarb once inherited a baseball team named the Loons, Miss Katzenbogen's expensive eccentricities on behalf of cats might have been shrugged off, but not on Laurel Canyon Boulevard.

Miss Katzenbogen had commissioned the renovations for what her neighbors called her cat house before learning that municipal zoning regulations imposed a limit of three cats per household. When she sought a belated exemption, 50 neighbors opposed her petition, arguing that the large number of cats would lower property values and even lure pet-eating coyotes into the neighborhood.

After Miss Katzenbogen gave assurances that cat litter would be removed daily and that the cats would be confined to their quarters and not loosed on the timorous neighborhood, she received an exemption allowing her to keep her 20 cats as long as they lived.

With the cats taken care of, she plunged into her new life, becoming a mainstay of several animal care agencies both as volunteer and philanthropist.

For all the time she devoted to cats in general and her cats in particular, Miss Katzenbogen managed to live a rich, full and varied life, indulging her passions for expensive clothes, movies and the arts and enjoying an active social life with a wide circle of friends.

If her extravagances on behalf of her cats raised eyebrows along the way, Miss Katzenbogen stood her ground.

"If I went out and bought a piece of jewelry or an expensive car, nobody would think twice or criticize me," she told The Los Angeles Times in 1992. "If I want to spend my money and take care of my cats, which are my family, I don't think it's anybody's business."

Aside from her father and aunt, Miss Katzenbogen, who never married, is survived only by her cats, all of whom, her animal adoption friends vowed, would be placed in loving homes, although none perhaps as loving and certainly not as luxurious as the one they have been accustomed to.

November 7, 1997

Nguyen Ngoc Loan, 67, Dies;

Executed Viet Cong Prisoner

Nguyen Ngoc Loan, the quick-tempered South Vietnamese national police commander whose impromptu execution of a Viet Cong prisoner on a Saigon street in the Tet offensive of 1968 helped galvanize American public opinion against the war, died on Tuesday at his home in Burke, Va. He was 67 and had operated a pizza parlor in nearby Dale City.

A son, Larry Nguyen, said the cause was cancer.

In a long war that claimed two million lives, the death of a single Viet Cong official would hardly have seemed noteworthy, especially in a week when thousands of insurgents were killed mounting an offensive that included the beheading of women and children in Saigon.

But when Brig. Gen. Nguyen Ngoc Loan raised his pistol on Feb. 1, 1968, extended his arm and fired a bullet through the head of the prisoner, who stood with his hands tied behind his back, the general did so in full view of an NBC cameraman and an Associated Press photographer.

And when the film was shown on television and the picture appeared on the front pages of newspapers around the world, the images created an immediate revulsion at a seemingly gratuitous act of savagery that was widely seen as emblematic of a seemingly gratuitous war.

The photograph, by Eddie Adams, was especially vivid, a frozen moment that put a wincing face of horror on the war. Taken almost at once with the squeeze of the trigger, the photo showed the prisoner, unidentified and wearing black shorts and a plaid shirt, in a final grimace as the bullet passed through his brain.

Close examination of the photo, which won a Pulitzer Prize in 1969, showed the slug leaving his head.

For all the emotional impact, the episode had little immediate influence on the tide of American involvement in the war, which continued seven years longer, until the evacuation of Saigon in 1975. Indeed, it was four years after the execution that another indelible image of the war created a new round of revulsion, the sight of a screaming 9-year-old as she ran naked along a road after having been burned in a South Vietnamese napalm attack.

The execution changed General Loan's life.

One of the 11 children of a prosperous mechanical engineer, Mr. Loan was born in Hue. He graduated near the top of his class at the University of Hue and begun a career as a jet pilot in the South Vietnamese Air Force. As a close friend of Nguyen Cao Ky, the swashbuckling pilot who became Premier in 1965, Mr. Loan, then a colonel, was put in charge of the national police and gained an immediate reputation among Western reporters for his temper and rages at the scenes of Viet Cong attacks on civilian targets.

(AP/Wide World Photos)

Some of those who knew him said General Loan would not have carried out the prisoner execution if reporters and photographers had not been at the scene.

Mr. Loan insisted that his action was justified because the prisoner had been the captain of a terrorist squad that had killed the family of one of his deputy commanders.

Even so, the killing and other summary executions by the South's military in the Tet offensive drew immediate rebukes from American officials. A few days after the incident, Mr. Ky, who had become Vice President, said the prisoner had not been in the Viet Cong military but was "a very high ranking" political official.

Mr. Loan later suggested that the execution had not been the rash act it might have appeared to be but had been carried out because a deputy commander he had ordered to shoot had hesitated. "I think, 'Then I must do it,'" he recounted. "If you hesitate, if you didn't do your duty, the men won't follow you."

Vo Suu, a cameraman at the scene for NBC News, recalled that immediately after the shooting the general had walked over to a reporter and said, "These guys kill a lot of our people, and I think Buddha will forgive me."

When General Loan was severely wounded while charging a Viet Cong hideout three months later and taken to Australia for treatment, there was such an outcry there against him that he was moved to the Walter Reed Army Medical Center in Washington, where he was repeatedly denounced in Congress.

Back in Saigon, Mr. Loan, who had been relieved of his command after having been wounded, seemed a changed man, devoting time to showering presents on orphans. At the fall of Saigon his pleas for American help in fleeing were ignored. But he and his family escaped in a South Vietnamese plane.

After his presence in the United States became known there was a move to deport him as a war criminal. But the efforts fizzled, and Mr. Loan, whose right leg had been amputated, settled in northern Virginia, where he eventually opened his pizzeria, which he operated until 1991 when publicity about his past led to a sharp decline in business. As a message scrawled on a restroom wall put it, "We know who you are."

In addition to his son, who also lives in Burke, Mr. Loan is survived by his wife, Chinh Mai; a daughter, Nguyen Anh of Fairfield, Va.; three other children, a number of brothers and sisters and nine grandchildren.

July 16, 1998

JACK BIBLO,

USED BOOKSELLER FOR HALF A CENTURY,

DIES AT 91

Jack Biblo, a bookish sort of man who spent a musty half century on Manhattan's Book Row as the founding proprietor of the Biblo & Tannen used, er antiquarian, bookstore on Fourth Avenue, then retired at 73 to open a smaller store around the corner from his home in Brooklyn Heights, died on June 5 at Long Island College Hospital in Brooklyn. He was 91 and until a couple of years ago had been active at the Biblo bookstore on Hicks Street.

It's been a while since the bustling stretch of Fourth Avenue from Eighth to 14th Streets had more than 30 stores specializing in rare, out-of-print or merely used books. It is a tribute to Biblo & Tannen's standing, not to mention the proprietors' foresight in buying their building in 1955, that when it finally closed in 1979 it was one of the few survivors of a storied tradition.

For someone who never fulfilled his dream of reading every book in the public library, Mr. Biblo had quite a run for himself. From the time he opened the first Biblo bookstore on 14th Street in 1928 until he and his partner, Jack Tannen, closed their last store, at 63 Fourth Avenue, between 9th and 10th Streets, he had helped sell hundreds of thousands of books and become something of a local institution.

Mr. Biblo also did quite well for someone whose formal schooling ended with the eighth grade, but then he received a remarkable advanced education at what it would be a shame not to call Biblo Tech. Which is to say he was at once self-taught and got all of his book learning by haunting New York public libraries.

To hear him tell it, Mr. Biblo, an East New York native whose original name was Biblowitz, could hardly have avoided developing a love of books growing up in a Brooklyn neighborhood that attracted Jewish immigrants of such passionate intellectual, social and cultural interests that when they weren't giving street corner speeches they would be boning up at the local library.

It was a tribute to Mr. Biblo's personal passion for reading that when he found the libraries in East New York and neighboring Brownsville too crowded for comfort he would walk to more deserted libraries in Ridgewood and other less bookish neighborhoods.

After leaving school Mr. Biblo held a series of odd jobs, among them working on a horse-drawn laundry wagon and as a waiter in the Catskills, but he preferred the leisurely life of reading, so much so that by the time he read his way up to the main branch of the New York Public Library, his mother provided the daily dime to cover his subway fares.

The son of a man who worked in distribution for the Hearst newspapers (but would not allow a copy of what he regarded as scurrilous yellow journalism into his home) Mr. Biblo later ran a

(Andy Feldman)

newsstand on 47th Street in Manhattan, did well enough to finance a three-month hitchhiking trip across the country, then returned determined to enter the book business.

Borrowing $300 from his mother, he opened his first store at age 22 on 14th Street in Manhattan and a few months later converted one of his regular customers, Jack Tannen, a tie salesman, into a full partner.

The two Jacks quickly became the odd couple of Book Row. Mr. Tannen, who died in 1991, was a highly gregarious sort, an aspiring actor who loved the limelight, while Mr. Biblo was almost a sobersides, a quiet, reserved man who provided a counterweight to his irrepressible partner.

In a notoriously marginal business, whose need for low rents made Fourth Avenue an ideal location, the partners had a rough going in the early days, often sleeping in their store overnight so they could get to the Salvation Army warehouse early enough to have their pick of the day's offerings before opening the store at 9 and keeping it open until midnight to squeeze in every available customer.

Like other stores at the time what kept Biblo & Tannen going during the Depression was a lucrative under-the-counter trade in what booksellers called erotica and the courts condemned as pornography.

The partners also developed an expertise in first editions, but while other stores specialized in specific areas, like art or music, their store, which eventually stocked 100,000 books, covered the waterfront.

Along the way the partners started a reprint publishing house, Canaveral Press, which specialized in reissues of works in the public domain but also issued previously unpublished works by Edgar Rice Burroughs, the creator of Tarzan, a Biblo favorite.

Indeed, after a flare-up of allergies, an occupational hazard of a musty business, forced Mr. Tannen to retire, and Mr. Biblo to open a smaller store that his wife Frances still operates in Brooklyn Heights, Mr. Biblo said reading every book in the public library was not his only unfulfilled ambition.

He had also, he said, dreamed of going to Africa to look for Tarzan.

In addition to his wife he is survived by a sister, Lillian Goodman of Baton Rouge, La., and a brother, Albert, of Miami.

June 18, 1998

Kay Halle, 93,

an Intimate of Century's Giants

Kay Halle, a glamorous Cleveland department store heiress who cut a heady swath through the 20th-century firmament, befriending and bewitching luminaries on both sides of the Atlantic and serving as a perceptive gadfly in politics, society and the arts, died on Aug. 7 at her home in Washington. She was 93.

During a remarkable life in which she formed enduring intimate relationships with George Gershwin, Randolph Churchill, W. Averell Harriman, Joseph P. Kennedy, Walter Lippmann, Buckminster Fuller and scores of other diverse figures, Miss Halle demonstrated such a flair for friendship and a knack for bringing people together that it is a wonder she found time for anything else.

She had a creditable enough career in journalism and with American intelligence in World War II. But Miss Halle, who wrote for The Cleveland Plain Dealer and other publications, conducted radio interviews with public figures and provided intermission commentary for Cleveland Orchestra broadcasts, was at her best in private settings.

A tall, slender, blonde beauty who kept her youthful good looks well beyond middle age and whose infectious enthusiasm continued long after that, Miss Halle (pronounced HAL-ee) once showed a friend a list of 64 men who had proposed to her, among them a youthful Randolph Churchill and an aging Averell Harriman.

(For all her reputation as a femme fatale, the "Mata Halle" nickname that William J. Donovan pinned on her during her years with his wartime Office of Strategic Services was more pun than analogy to the World War I seductress.)

Given the range and ardor of her admirers, one of Miss Halle's more notable achievements may have been avoiding marriage and thriving in an era when even independently wealthy spinsters were viewed with suspicion.

Seeking safety in numbers, she became famous for surprising wealthy suitors by showing up for dinner dates with several less well-heeled admirers in tow.

Even more notable was the fact that she remained on such good terms with her spurned suitors. Thirty years and two marriages after he was first rejected, for example, Mr. Churchill was still as devoted to her as ever.

That was partly because Miss Halle was such an attentive listener that she could repeat entire conversations verbatim, making her a reliable and entertaining gossip.

For all that, she had such a passion for discretion that long after most of her paramours were dead, including those who had not been free to propose marriage, she refused all entreaties to write her memoirs. Even intimates who are certain, for example, that she had been Joseph Kennedy's favorite mistress cannot say for sure whether her friendship with Gershwin, who wrote her gushing letters, had been a full-fledged romance.

A product of a fairy-tale union between a wealthy German-Jewish merchant and an Irish-Catholic working girl, Miss Halle, whose father was a founder of the old Halle Brothers department store in Cleveland, grew up in an ecumenical, intellectually charged atmosphere that left her without prejudice or pretension and with an eclectic range of interests, especially in people.

Her survivors include a sister, Ann Little of Chagrin Falls, Ohio.

Making the most of her family connections and even more of those she formed on her own, Miss Halle got her start in political society early. During a family visit to Washington when she was 13, President Woodrow Wilson's Secretary of War, Newton D. Baker, a former Cleveland mayor, had a young assistant, Walter Lippmann, show her around. He got her admitted to a special session of Congress, making her perhaps the last person alive to have witnessed Wilson's request for a declaration of war in April 1917.

Later, after one boring year at Smith College, Miss Halle took New York by storm, captivating Gershwin and making her apartment a headquarters of the roaring 20's.

She broadened her scope considerably after Randolph Churchill gave a speech in Cleveland in 1931 and fell in love with her. Although Miss Halle, who was eight years older than he was, kept him at bay, she became a frequent visitor to Chartwell, the Churchill country home in England, and a favorite of his father, Sir Winston Churchill.

As a result, Miss Halle, who was an old friend of Franklin D. Roosevelt and campaigned for him in 1932, became one of the few people to be on intimate family terms with the two wartime leaders.

Miss Halle, who made Washington her base after World War II, became such a Churchill enthusiast that she published two volumes of his collected sayings and was credited with using her considerable drawing room influence to persuade Congress to confer the honorary American citizenship that he considered his most prized public tribute.

August 24, 1997

HALLIE C. STILLWELL,

A RANCHER AND TEXAS LEGEND,

DIES AT 99

Hallie Crawford Stillwell, who drove a covered wagon into Alpine, Tex., in 1910, worked as a teacher and then settled down and became a Big Bend legend as a sharp-shooting ranch wife on horseback, died on Monday at an Alpine hospital, two months and two days shy of her 100th birthday.

As a rough rancher, chatty newspaper columnist, justice of the peace, chili cook-off queen and mistress of a museum devoted to her life, Mrs. Stillwell, who was known as Miss Hallie far beyond the sweeping curve of the Rio Grande, became a Texas tourist attraction.

A native of Waco whose restless father kept the family on the move, including three years homesteading in the New Mexico Territory, she was 13 when she hitched up a four-horse team, gathered the reins and led a Conestoga convoy that took her family to the dusty little town of Alpine in the Big Bend region of southwestern Texas.

Six years later she received a teaching certificate, strapped on a six-shooter and set out for the town of Presidio on the Rio Grande, a major crossing point for Pancho Villa's raiders. When her father accused her of going off on a wild-goose chase, she stood her ground. "I'll gather my geese," she said, a retort that established her independence and provided the title for an autobiography.

After a year of dodging Mexican raiding parties and fending off drunken American soldiers, she took a safer position in Marathon, some distance from the border. Her father was relieved, until she decided to marry Roy Stillwell.

Though Mr. Stillwell owned a 22,000-acre spread 45 miles south of Marathon, he was a taciturn, hard-drinking, poker-playing widower more than twice her age. He may not have seemed a suitable husband, but the first time he drove up in his sporty Hudson Super Six, she later explained, "He decided he liked me, and I decided I liked that car."

Assuring her father that "I'd rather be an old man's darlin' than a young man's slave," she married Mr. Stillwell in 1918. She was 20 and he was 40.

After a honeymoon in San Antonio, Mr. Stillwell, whose first wife had not been the ranching sort and had lived in town, took his bride home and proudly showed off the 12-by-16-foot one-room cabin where he had lived for years with three crusty and decidedly misogynist ranch hands.

Meager as it was, the cabin had all the comforts of a bridal home except an actual bed. The couple slept on a bedroll on the floor, and Mrs. Stillwell had to be up and dressed by dawn to avoid being trampled by the cowboys trooping in to fix breakfast.

The hands, miffed enough at being displaced to the barn, were not about to let a woman meddle in the manly work of cowboy cooking. As it happened, they did not mind her performing such ladylike chores as riding herd on the cattle, wrestling calves to the ground for branding and shooting deer and other game for the table, especially after they discovered that she was a better shot than they were.

Not that they had any choice. Because the ranch was only 23 miles from the border and well within bandito-raiding range, it was considered unsafe to leave her home alone even though her husband kept a rifle in each corner of the house.

One day, after she proved her prowess as a marksman, Mrs. Stillwell, who rode with a .45 strapped to her waist and a 30.06 rifle slung across her saddle horn, was allowed to stay behind. It proved to be a disaster. Responding to some pent-up urge, she spent the day scrubbing an accumulation of charcoal graffiti off the cabin walls and used sand to scour the coffeepot until it gleamed inside and out.

After the cowboys returned and discovered that she had erased years of ranch records, they never let her forget it. "Washed any walls lately?" they would ask. They were more distressed at what she had done to their lovingly seasoned coffeepot. The coffee, they reminded her for years, was not fit to drink for six months.

As the babies started coming, a couple of bedrooms were added, and while her three children were in school, Mrs. Stillwell would even spend the week in town, but on weekends and in summers she continued to ride with her husband.

After her husband died in 1948, she soldiered on alone until 1964, when she turned the ranch over to her two sons and moved to Alpine, where she became justice of the peace for the Connecticut-sized Brewster County.

The work included serving as coroner, a job, she noted, she had mastered by observation as a teenager after watching a sheriff and his deputy cut down a challenger in a gunfight. Soon, she said, a man in a black coat strode up, took one look at the bloody remains, said, "He's dead," then whirled on his heel and left.

In recent years, Mrs. Stillwell had lived in a mobile home on the edge of the ranch where her daughter established a park for recreational vehicles with a replica of the cabin room she lived in as a bride in the 1920's.

In addition to regaling tourists, she worked on a sequel to "I'll Gather My Geese," her autobiography. Now being completed by a granddaughter, it is titled, "My Goose Is Cooked."

Mrs. Stillwell is survived by two sons, Roy and Guy, and a daughter, Dadie, all of the Big Bend region; a sister, Glen Harris of Presidio; 9 grandchildren; 15 great-grandchildren and 2 great-great-grandchildren.

August 24, 1997

Marshall Berger, 77,

Linguist with a Keen Ear

for an Accent

Marshall D. Berger, a latter-day Henry Higgins who taught generations of Noo Yawkahs how not to speak the Kings County English, died on May 28 at a hospital near his home in Orangeburg, N.Y. He was 77 and had taught speech at City College from 1946 to 1982.

His daughter Karen Berger said the cause was a stroke.

Although he taught a variety of speech courses, including debate and public presentation, Mr. Berger specialized in taking foreign students or natives with pronounced Brooklyn, Bronx or other distinct accents and teaching them how to speak more or less mainstream English.

A specialist in dialect geography, or dialectology, as it is known in linguistics, he was a dialectologist's dialectologist, a man with such a keen ear for the subtle variations of speech patterns that after listening for a few moments he could often tell a speaker's ethnic background, the neighborhood where he had grown up and his level of education.

And if he could not always identify the exact Brooklyn block, say, where a student had learned to play stickball, or just which of the Five Towns of Long Island he had moved to as a teenager, he came close enough often enough to awe his students.

Mr. Berger, a native of Buffalo, developed his interest in speech through a boyhood ambition to be a radio announcer. On a visit to a radio station, he was told that announcers need to overcome regional accents, an admonishment that impressed him so much that by the time he moved to Brooklyn at 13 he was well on his way to becoming an expert.

In addition to the myriad variations of American English, Mr. Berger was adept at foreign languages, working as a German translator with the Army Signal Corps in Germany during World War II.

It was the influx of veterans studying on the G.I. Bill that got him his academic start, leading him to become a tutor at City College, his alma mater, while studying for his doctorate at Columbia University.

Mr. Berger published one book, "Russian in a Nutshell," and turned out a stream of papers for journals like Word, the publication of the International Linguistic Association.

One reason, perhaps, that Mr. Berger, a former president of the association, did not do more writing was that he regarded teaching as his real calling, so much so that it did not much matter what he taught.

As his daughter recalled yesterday, he spent hours every week coaching her and her sister on their schoolwork, going so far as to teach himself the New Math as they learned it, and not resting until both had obtained doctorates of their own.

Perhaps the best evidence of Mr. Berger's skill as a teacher is that in his spare time he taught navigation for the Coast Guard Auxiliary even though he never owned a boat.

A man who made it a point to read his morning newspaper cover to cover, Mr. Berger seemed determined to know everything about everything. If that is impossible, he made such a run at it that his daughters and their husbands, all Ph.D.'s, developed a family game called "Stump Marshall," in a usually vain effort to ask him a question he could not answer.

It is understandable that they steered clear of his field, for when it came to dialect geography, Mr. Berger had few peers. It was he, for example, who developed a table of telltale words to determine an American's place of origin. People who grow up on the Eastern seaboard, for example, tend to distinguish the pronunciations of Mary, marry, and merry, while those born farther inland gradually lose the distinctions to the point that by Michigan all three are pronounced merry.

As for the vaunted Brooklyn accent, Mr. Berger helped establish that there are actually several variations, each so close to the others that some of his fellow linguists had to listen to recordings several times before being able to tell them apart.

Not content to recognize a Brooklyn accent, Mr. Berger drew on his broader knowledge of American speech and history to develop a theory of just how the signature "Toidy-toid Street" evolved. It was, he theorized, a result of the close commercial connections with the pre–Civil War South in which upper-class Southern speech, primarily from New Orleans and Charleston, S.C., was imported and hammered down to a lower-class Brooklynese.

In addition to his daughter, of Ossining, N.Y., Mr. Berger is survived by his wife, Gale; another daughter, Victoria Berger-Gross of Riverdale, the Bronx, and five grandchildren.

June 4, 1997

Philip O'Connor, 81,

Acerbic Memoirist, Dies

Philip O'Connor, an incorrigible, flamboyant and decidedly self-absorbed British eccentric who turned a fulsomely frank account of his abject childhood and misspent youth into a rollicking literary sensation in 1958, died on Friday at his home near Uzes in southern France. He was 81 and the author of "Memoirs of a Public Baby."

During a life in which he dabbled in painting and poetry, turned out a series of published and unpublished works, flirted with Communism, did a turn as a radio interviewer, succumbed to a succession of adoring women and supported himself largely by sponging off friends and various of his six wives, Mr. O'Connor wrote incessantly, mainly about himself.

The material, at least, was there.

By his own account in "Memoirs," which covered the first 25 years of his life, Mr. O'Connor was lucky to survive his childhood with a sense of humor, albeit a distinctly acerbic one.

The son of a well-educated Irish father he never knew and a woman of mixed Irish and Burmese ancestry whose aristocratic tastes exceeded her reach, he was born in Leighton Buzzard in Bedfordshire and taken almost immediately to France, where his mother abandoned him for two years in the care of a woman who ran a pastry shop.

When he was 7 his mother reclaimed him, took him back to England and then, after setting up housekeeping in a Soho cellar, abandoned him again, this time, he recounted, to the care of a one-legged bachelor civil servant who lived in a hut in Surrey.

Leaving school at 17, Mr. O'Connor plunged into the bohemian life in the artistic quarter of London known as Fitzrovia, declaiming doggerel at bars frequented by Dylan Thomas and others, giving impassioned, if not always comprehensible, speeches at Hyde Park Corner, tramping across England and Ireland and receiving treatment at a mental hospital for schizophrenia, a possibly erroneous diagnosis of a condition later aggravated by chronic alcoholism.

Along the way he took up with a woman who earned her living taking baths with older men, then improved his lot by marrying a wealthy woman who financed a high-living fling that ended when her money and her sanity ran out. (After she tried to kill him, she was confined to a mental hospital and Mr. O'Connor went on to charm other women.)

Mr. O'Connor, who began his literary career turning out surrealistic poetry, also took to buttonholing literary lions, not always to their delight.

He once sent a note up to Aldous Huxley's hotel suite demanding five pounds and on another occasion jumped out from behind a door and shouted "Boo!" at T. S. Eliot.

One literary figure who did not shrink from such antics was Stephen Spender, who wrote an admiring introduction to "Memoirs" and another when the book was reissued by Norton in 1989.

The book, hailed for its uncompromising honesty, was greeted in England with almost unremitting acclaim, which included an entire BBC broadcast devoted to its merits and lavish praise from Cyril Connolly and Philip Toynbee.

The book eventually drew praise from the disparate likes of Saul Bellow, Paul Bowles, Joseph Brodsky, William Burroughs, Arthur Miller and Dorothy Parker, but generally the appreciation on this side of the Atlantic was not unremitting.

Indeed, the daily book reviewer for The New York Times, Orville Prescott, couldn't seem to decide which he loathed more, the "sickening book" or the "sick man" who had produced it.

Mr. O'Connor, who emerged from his childhood with a lifelong disdain for the British middle class, fared better in the Times's Sunday Book Review, where John W. Aldrige, a professor of literature at New York University, likened Mr. O'Connor to Yeats, praised him for his "sharply epigrammatic wittiness" and hailed him for revealing himself as "an unspeakable cad, scoundrel and snob—in short a brutally honest man."

Two autobiographical sequels, "The Lower View" (1960), about bicycle visits to writers and artists, and "Living in Croesor" (1962), describing his sojourn in a Welsh village, were less well received. But "Vagrancy" (1963), a study of those on the bottom of British society, enjoyed a vogue on university reading lists.

During the early 1960's Mr. O'Connor conducted a series of radio interviews with drug addicts, alcoholics and other misfits, including Quentin Crisp, the flamboyant eccentric who credited Mr. O'Connor with inventing him.

By 1967 Mr. O'Connor professed to find life in Britain so stultifying that when he caught the eye of Panna Grady, a wealthy New York woman 20 years his junior, he allowed her to take him to a comfortable refuge in France, where he lived for the rest of his life, writing thousands of letters to friends, often with abject apologies for past hurts, and keeping a daily journal that runs to millions of words.

He is survived by his companion, Mrs. Grady; his daughter Allaye, also of Uzes; seven other children and eight grandchildren.

June 4, 1998

TOOTS BARGER, 85,

THE QUEEN OF DUCKPINS' WOBBLY WORLD

Toots Barger, a perennial world champion in a decidedly regional sport, died on Monday at a retirement home in Frederick, Md. She was 85 and had long been known as the Queen of Duckpins.

Her family said the cause was cancer.

If duckpins doesn't ring a bell, chances are you didn't grow up in or around Baltimore, where the squat-pin version of the familiar 10-pin bowling game was invented and became something of a municipal mania.

During the years Mrs. Berger was virtually invincible, from the mid-1940's to the mid-1960's, the sport was so popular in Baltimore that the prestigious annual tournament sponsored by The Baltimore Evening Sun was regularly broadcast on local television, and Mrs. Barger, who won the tournament 12 times in 22 years, became such an acclaimed figure that she was regarded as the city's premier athlete until Johnny Unitas came to town.

If the former Mary Elizabeth Ryan's record of 13 world duckpin championships and 9 world scoring records doesn't sound impressive, it's a safe bet you haven't stood at the head of a regulation, 60-foot bowling lane and tried to knock down 10 undersized (9-inch tall) pins placed at the usual 12 inches spacing with a 3-pound ball just 5 inches in diameter.

If you had, you would not be surprised that in her reign in duckpins, which has the same 10-frame scoring system as regular bowling and the same theoretic perfect score of 300, Mrs. Barger dominated the sport's women's division for the better part of two decades without ever once reaching 200.

But then one of duckpins' chief appeals has been that scoring is so difficult that while there have been myriad perfect games in regular bowling, no one has ever rolled a perfect game in tournament duckpins, whose highest recorded score is 279. (Mrs. Barger's best game was 198.)

No wonder. In contrast to the 8.5-inch bowling ball, the duckpin ball is small enough to roll between any two pins with plenty of room to spare. As a result, even though duckpins has been called a game of spares in contrast to bowling as a game of strikes, a spare (knocking down all 10 pins in two rolls) is so difficult that a third ball is allowed when a spare has not been scored.

Because the lightweight duckpin ball, which has no finger holes, is small enough for a child to handle, duckpins has long been cherished as a family sport in Baltimore.

Even so, Mrs. Barger, a Baltimore native who was given her nickname by an aunt, seems not to have played the sport as a child, perhaps because she was born only 13 years after duckpins' storied beginning.

(WM Klender, The Baltimore Sun)

According to Baltimore legend, it was invented in 1900 in an upstairs bowling alley at a tavern owned by two of Baltimore's premier sports heroes, the baseball figures John J. McGraw and Wilbert Robinson.

The game got its name, so the story goes, because the squat, cutdown pins reminded the duck-shooting owners of ducks.

Mrs. Barger, whose husband, Ernest, was a plumber who later operated a bowling alley managed by his wife, was the mother of two children when she joined a housewife's duckpin league in the late 1930's and discovered that she had a rare talent for a difficult game.

Primarily because she played with dead solid oak balls in the days before the lively plastic pin era, Mrs. Barger's records have long since been eclipsed, and the sport itself, which once proliferated along the Atlantic coast from New Hampshire to North Carolina and as far inland as Indiana, has been in serious decline, even in Baltimore.

Even so, Mrs. Barger continued playing until three years ago and remained such a well-known figure that in 1992 she achieved renewed prominence leading a campaign to have duckpins named the Maryland state sport.

The campaign failed, perhaps because legislators felt duckpins was just too odd to be the state sport, especially when Maryland already had an official sport: jousting.

Mrs. Barger is survived by a son, Ernest Jr., of La Jolla, Calif.; a daughter, Mary Jane Joyce of Derwood, Md.; four grandchildren and six great-grandchildren.

October 2, 1998

EDGAR NOLLNER, 94, DIES;

HERO IN EPIDEMIC

It was one of the great cliff-hangers of the 20th century, one that held a nation in white-knuckled thrall for more than a week in 1925 as the world wondered whether a supply of life-saving serum would make it to icebound Nome, Alaska, in time to save the town's 1,429 residents from a raging diphtheria epidemic.

Now, almost three-quarters of a century later, an event that dominated radio broadcasts and newspaper headlines is a fading memory.

The tale has often been told, but when Edgar Nollner died on Monday at his home in Galena, Alaska, it seemed time to tell it once more: Mr. Nollner, who was 94, was the last of the 20 intrepid mushers and more than 150 dogs who became national heroes when they made their way in relays through raging storms over 674 forbidding miles to save a town and carve a legend in the snow.

The race against death, as it was called, inspired statues and speeches and eventually the annual Iditarod dog sled race, but to Mr. Nollner it was simply a day's work.

The son of a Missouri man who came over the Chilkoot Pass for the 1890's gold rush, Mr. Nollner, whose mother was an Athabascan Indian, was born 10 miles upriver in Old Village, but from the age of 15 he made his home and his living in the Yukon River town of Galena.

He was 20 when the call went out for the territory's best dog sledders to form a relay from the railhead at Nenana to Nome. Like the others, he was an experienced musher who carried the mail and other supplies by dog sled, raced and used his sled to haul wood and carry home the area's abundant game.

It was on Jan. 21 that the first ominous Morse code message from Dr. Curtis Welch, Nome's only physician and the head of the Public Health Service's most remote outpost, clacked out over radiotelegraph to "Outside," as Alaskans called the rest of the world.

Reporting several cases of diphtheria, a highly contagious and often fatal respiratory ailment, and two deaths, Dr. Welch, who was rapidly using up Nome's 7,500 units of six-year-old antitoxin, issued an urgent appeal for more of the serum, the only hope, he warned, of averting a full-scale epidemic in a community whose large Eskimo population had proved vulnerable to alien diseases.

A supply of 300,000 units, enough to cure about 100 patients or treat perhaps 300 exposed to the disease, was swiftly traced to the Anchorage Railroad Hospital, but the question was how to get it the 1,000 miles to Nome.

Delivery by air seemed the obvious answer, but with Alaska's only two planes, both open-cockpit models, crated for the winter, the territorial Governor, Scott C. Bone, knew such an effort would be futile—and in the frigid, windy weather almost certainly fatal. He was willing enough to let pilots risk their lives, but he would not risk the serum.

So, turning to a more reliable, 19th-century technology, he ordered the serum sent by rail from Anchorage to Nenana, 298 miles to the north. From there, it would be a matter of men and their dogs.

The train arrived at Nenana at 10:30 P.M. on the 27th, and the fur-wrapped 20-pound cylinder was handed over to Wild Bill Shannon, who lashed it to his sled, called out to his malamutes and set off down the frozen Tanana River into history.

At a time when Nome received almost all of its winter supplies by dog sled, it normally took a musher 15 to 20 days to make the trip over the old Iditarod Trail, and never less than 9. But with 20 mushers and dog teams dividing the trek into short sprints, the serum flew across the territory, arriving in Nome on Feb. 2 in a record 5 days and 7 hours.

Mr. Nollner, who had the 10th leg, had been scheduled to take a 42-mile run, but when his married younger brother, George, asked for a role, he let him drive the last 18 miles.

Like others, Mr. Nollner, who ran his leg at night, covering the 24 miles from Whiskey Point to Galena in three hours, reported so much blowing snow that he could not see his dogs but really did not need to. The dogs, led by his trusty Dixie, knew the trail and never faltered.

Mr. Nollner's friend Charlie Evans did not fare as well. On his 30-mile run from Bishop Mountain to Nulato, Mr. Evans's two lead dogs froze to death in harness, so he did the obvious thing—he took their place and pulled along with his other dogs on the final miles of the run.

Within days after the serum arrived in Nome (frozen but quickly thawed), the epidemic, which claimed five lives, had been broken.

The 20 men and scores of dogs on the famed serum run were all hailed as heroes, but to most students of the event, the Norwegian-born Leonhard Seppala and his lead dog, a 48-pound Siberian husky named Togo, were the most heroic, because they traveled the first and longest leg of the run, 260 miles, before handing off the serum. But much of the credit ended up going to a second-string lead dog on the final 55-mile leg, Balto, whose background was garbled with Togo's in glowing news reports of the day. A statue of BALTO, the subject of a children's book and a 1995 animated movie, stands in Central Park, and his stuffed body has been exhibited at museums in Cleveland and Anchorage.

For all the acclaim it received, the serum run marked the end of an era. Before the year was over, Alaska's scheduled air service and the proliferation of snow machines brought an end to mushing as an essential north country occupation. The Iditarod, a network of interconnecting trails extending for more than 2,000 miles, was soon abandoned until parts of it were revived in 1973 for the annual race. And if the threat of diphtheria now seems quaint, it is only because the serum run brought an end to the disease as a health menace in the United States.

To Mr. Nollner, a treasured fixture at the modern Iditarod race, greeting the mushers as they came through Galena, the serum run was just part of a lifetime in the wild.

A man who recalled when caribou, beavers, foxes and wolverines abounded, and the springtime skies would be so black with migrating geese that a single shot could feed a family for a month, he continued to live the outdoor life. A gregarious sort who was widely admired, he was always the life of the party at the great north country potlatch celebrations, and he liked dancing almost as much as he did hunting.

Along the way, he married twice and fathered two dozen children, 20 of whom survive, along with what some of them insist are more than 200 grandchildren and no telling how many great-grandchildren.

Despite the end of the dog sled era, Mr. Nollner did not abandon his dogs and sleds right away. Nor did he abandon saving lives.

In February 1953, while gathering wood with his dog team, he heard an Air Force plane crash. Finding two wounded officers on the verge of freezing to death in temperatures 54 degrees below zero, he built a fire and called his friend Charlie Evans to help him get them to town. A quarter-century later when one of the officers, Lionel Levin, tracked him down, Mr. Nollner told him it had simply been a day's work.

January 24, 1999

CORRECTION: Because of an editing error, an obituary on Sunday about Edgar Noller, the last of the 20 mushers who carried life-saving serum 674 miles to Nome, Alaska, in a diphtheria epidemic in 1925, misstated the distance covered by another, Leonhard Seppala. He and his lead dog, Togo, ran the 18th leg, not the first. They covered 91 miles (260 miles was the total distance they traveled, including a 169-mile run from Nome to the start of their relay leg).

Marguerite Young, 87,
Author and Icon, Dies

Marguerite Young, the Indiana-born writer who became a darling
of the avant-garde and inspired a devoted cult following even as
she infuriated and confounded mainstream critics with a single
gargantuan novel, died on Friday at the home of a niece in Indianapolis. She was 87.

Miss Young, a longtime New School writing teacher who
began her literary career as an award-winning poet and ended it
as a critic, essayist and biographer, was a respected literary figure
and cherished Greenwich Village eccentric well before Scribners
published her one and only novel, "Miss MacIntosh, My Darling,"
in 1965.

Afterward she became a legend: the woman with the pageboy
haircut who looked like W. H. Auden, wrote like James Joyce,
strode through the Village in her signature serapes, had breakfast
at Bigelow's with Richard Wright, got drunk at the White Horse
Tavern with Dylan Thomas, palled around with Truman Capote
and Carson McCullers, kept a vast collection of dolls in her
Bleecker Street apartment and regaled intimates with tales of her
romantic conquests.

But for all her range, Miss Young drew a line. By her own
account, she welcomed the advances of the poet Allen Tate but
rebuffed those of Miss McCullers, telling her at Yaddo in 1946,
"Well, Carson, if I could love any woman, it would be you."

Anyone who has not heard of Miss Young, nor read her mag-
num opus, "Miss MacIntosh, My Darling," need not feel ashamed.
Surely one of the most widely unread books ever acclaimed, it has

actually been read by comparatively few; by fewer still all the way through.

Indeed, even Miss Young's most ardent admirers (and her admirers, from Anaïs Nin and Djuna Barnes to John Gardner, Anne Tyler and a prolific band of feminists, tend to be ardent) concede that the book, variously described as "a mammoth epic," "a massive fable" and "a work of stunning magnitude and beauty" (not to mention "hallucinatory," "ethereal" and "utterly stupefying"), is rather much to take in a single season. Too rich for a repast, it is better savored, they say, like a bedside dish of candy, one bite-sized bonbon at a time.

It is "Miss MacIntosh," sure enough, that the hero of Miss Tyler's "Accidental Tourist" carries with him to dip into for consolation from time to time.

It is a reflection of the book's decidedly mixed reception that while the daily review in The New York Times dismissed it with a sneer, Miss Young's friend, William Goyen, turned a Times Sunday review into a page-long paean.

Narrated by the aptly named Vera Cartwheel, who indulges in nonstop verbal and mental gymnastics during a 948-page bus ride from coastal New England to the heartland of America—and the interior of the author's mind—it describes the narrator's largely imaginary quest for the illusory truth about her childhood nursemaid, Miss MacIntosh, who is bald, single-breasted and may or may not have drowned when Miss Cartwheel was 14 years old.

Those who have merely read about "Miss MacIntosh" know it chiefly as a matter of length, from the 18 years it took to write to its very heft. At 1,198 pages and some three-quarters of a million words, it has been described as the longest novel in English ever published in a single volume; later editions, including a facsimile reissue by Dalkey last year, have split it in two.

Miss Young, who was born in Indianapolis in 1908, was precocious. She wrote her first poems when she was 6, joined the Authors League at 11, published her first poem at Indiana University when she was 19, won first prize in a literary contest at Butler University when she was 20 and published her first book of poems, "Prismatic Ground," at 28, in 1937, a year after receiving a master's in Elizabethan and Jacobean literature from the University of Chicago.

Her most significant formative experiences at Chicago seem to have occurred outside the classroom, among them the friendships she struck up with Thornton Wilder, Gertrude Stein and other literary figures, but most notably her part-time job reading to a wealthy addict, Minna Weissenbach, a patron of Edna St. Vincent Millay. Miss Weissenbach and her astonishing flights of drug-induced fantasy inspired the famous "opium lady" in "Miss MacIntosh."

Although she shunned drugs, Miss Young was capable of some pretty astonishing mental flights of her own, both on and off the printed page. In her (more or less) real life, as she told Charles Ruas in an interview included in his "Conversations with American Writers" (Knopf, 1985), she would regularly startle her New School students by announcing that, say, Henry James had suddenly arrived in the classroom.

And the Greenwich Village she inhabited was a far more interesting place than the one perceived by most:

"I see Emily Dickinson quite often," she told Mr. Ruas, "Virginia Woolf, and Dickens. Poe, oh, all the time. I see him on misty nights at Sheridan Square when the rain's falling. He's going into a little cigar store to get a cigar. I am on very close terms with Poe."

Miss Young, who taught at an Indianapolis high school and at the University of Iowa after Chicago, moved to New York in 1943 and burst on the literary scene two years later with the simultaneous publication of "Moderate Fable," which won the best poetry award from the National Academy of Arts and Letters, and "Angel in the Forest," a highly acclaimed account of successive utopian communities at New Harmony, Ind.

After the publication of "Miss MacIntosh," in 1965, she began writing "Harp Song for a Radical," a biography of Eugene V. Debs. Thirty years later the book is yet to be published, but Victoria Wilson, an editor at Knopf, said yesterday the "astonishing" work needs just a little more pruning.

It seems the manuscript Miss Young turned in was 2,500 pages long.

She leaves no immediate survivors.

November 20, 1995

Rev. Louis Saunders, 88, Dies;

Buried Oswald

The Rev. Louis A. Saunders, who spent half a century as such a quietly dedicated minister, missionary and religious official that he became known chiefly for a single, instinctive act of Christian duty, died on April 5 at his home in suburban Dallas. He was 88 and the man who gave Lee Harvey Oswald a Christian burial.

Mr. Saunders, a native of Richlands, N.C., whose father and two uncles were ministers of the Christian Church (Disciples of Christ), graduated from Johnson Bible College in Tennessee, studied theology at Duke and received his divinity degree from Vanderbilt University.

He left an Arkansas church after Pearl Harbor to join the Army, completing chaplain's school at Harvard, and participated in the Normandy invasion. He ended up in the Philippines after agreeing to swap assignments so a married colleague could remain close to his children.

After the war, Mr. Saunders stayed in the Philippines as a missionary, building the first high school in a remote Luzon Province and impressed a young Presbyterian missionary by taking her six plants of cascading orchids wrapped in banana leaves.

A few years later, while both were studying theology in New York, they were married. After receiving his master's in a joint Columbia-Union Theological Seminary program, Mr. Saunders served briefly as pastor of a church in Baywater, Tex., before becoming executive director in 1957 of the Fort Worth Council of Churches, an interdenominational group that coordinated social and other programs.

Six years later, when he learned that President John F. Kennedy's presumed assassin, Lee Harvey Oswald, who had been killed by Jack Ruby, was to be buried in Fort Worth, Mr. Saunders knew his duty.

Even as he was leading the arrangements for an interdenominational memorial service for the slain President, Mr. Saunders worked the phones to make sure that a minister would be present when Mr. Oswald was buried at Rose Hill Cemetery on the outskirts of Fort Worth.

Assured that two Lutheran ministers had agreed to conduct the service at the request of Mr. Oswald's mother, Marguerite, a Lutheran and resident of Fort Worth, Mr. Saunders went to the cemetery as an observer.

It was only after he had made his way through the throngs at the cemetery gates that Mr. Saunders learned that the ministers, objecting to an open-air ceremony where they would be exposed to potential snipers, had not appeared.

When Mr. Oswald's mother asked him to fill in, Mr. Saunders obliged. He had left his Bible in his car, but as the small, forlorn Oswald family looked on from a row of folding chairs, he recited the 23d Psalm ("The Lord is my shepherd . . .") and a passage from John 14 ("In my father's house are many mansions . . .") from memory, and delivered one of the briefest eulogies ever:

"Mrs. Oswald tells me that her son, Lee Harvey, was a good boy and that she loved him. And today, Lord, we commit his spirit to Your divine care."

Within weeks his gesture had prompted an outpouring of financial support for the impoverished Oswald family.

Mr. Saunders went on to become executive director of the Council of Churches in Dallas, where he created a ministry at the county jail, expanded a ministry at Parkland Memorial Hospital and helped soothe the way for racial desegregation.

After his ostensible retirement in 1976, he served as interim minister at five churches.

In addition to his wife, Jeanne, he is survived by a daughter, Susan, of Carrollton, Tex.; two sons, John, of Coppell, Tex., and James, of Dallas; two brothers, John, of Dinwiddie, Va., and Ken, of Winston-Salem, N.C., and a grandchild.

April 17, 1998

Douglas Corrigan, 88, Dies;

Wrong-Way Trip Was the Right Way

to Celebrity as an Aviator

Douglas Corrigan, a brash, errant aviator who captured the imagination of a Depression-weary public in 1938 when he took off from Brooklyn on a nonstop solo flight to Los Angeles and landed his improbable airplane in Dublin a day later, died on Saturday at a hospital in Orange, Calif. He was 88 and had been lionized for more than half a century as Wrong Way Corrigan.

The few people who were at Floyd Bennett Field when Mr. Corrigan took off at 5:15 on the morning of July 17, 1938, were baffled when the 31-year-old aviator turned into a cloud bank and disappeared to the east.

According to his flight plan, he should have been heading west.

As they and the world learned when his jerry-built, overloaded secondhand airplane touched down at Dublin's Baldonnel Airport 28 hours and 13 minutes later, Mr. Corrigan had not only known what he was doing, he had also flown straight into the hearts of the American people.

"I'm Douglas Corrigan," he told a group of startled Irish airport workers who gathered around him when he landed. "Just got in from New York. Where am I? I intended to fly to California."

Although he continued to claim with a more or less straight face that he had simply made a wrong turn and been led astray by a faulty compass, the story was far from convincing, especially to the American aviation authorities who had rejected his repeated requests to make just such a flight because his modified 1929

Curtiss-Robin monoplane was judged unworthy of more than an experimental aircraft certification.

Unmoved by evidence that he had not checked weather reports for the North Atlantic before his flight and had carried charts showing only his supposedly planned route to California, the authorities deemed his plane so unsafe and his flight so illegal that it took a 600-word official telegram to detail all the regulations he had violated.

But if Mr. Corrigan had such a twinkle in his eye when he told his story that he appeared to be trying to suppress a wink, the authorities had trouble stifling a wink of their own.

Although his pilot's license was instantly suspended, Mr. Corrigan, who returned to the United States by ship, did not miss a minute of flying time. He served the entire suspension at sea. The license was reinstated as soon as he and his crated-up plane sailed into New York Harbor aboard the liner Manhattan on Aug. 4, and received a tumultuous greeting.

There was an even larger welcome the next day when an estimated one million New Yorkers lined lower Broadway for a ticker-tape parade that eclipsed the one given for Charles A. Lindbergh after his solo flight to Paris in 1927.

Mr. Corrigan's 3,150-mile flight was an immediate sensation, pushing depressing economic news and grim international reports aside on the front pages of American newspapers and dominating radio broadcasts across the country.

Although half a dozen well-known pilots, among them Amelia Earhart and Wylie Post, had made solo flights across the Atlantic since Lindbergh had blazed the trail in the Spirit of St. Louis in 1927, none struck such a chord with the American people as Mr. Corrigan did.

That was partly because he was seen as an engaging and impish young pilot who had boldly thumbed his nose at authority, then baldly denied it, and partly because he had made the flight not in a state of the art aircraft with cutting edge instruments, but in a rickety plane so precariously patched together that it was variously dubbed an airborne crate and a flying jalopy.

Among other things, Mr. Corrigan, who had bought the plane in New York as a wreck for $310 in 1935 and nursed it cow pasture by cow pasture back to California, had ripped out the original 90-horsepower engine and replaced it with a 165-horsepower model cobbled together from two old Wright engines. He had also installed five extra fuel tanks, which completely blocked his forward view, and various parts, including the cabin door, were held together with baling wire.

Mr. Corrigan, who was born in Galveston, Tex., and grew up in Los Angeles, had been dreaming of a flight across the Atlantic for a long time. Enchanted with aviation at an early age, he had become a barnstorming pilot, flying instructor and an aviation mechanic who helped build Lindbergh's Spirit of St. Louis in San Diego. It was Mr. Corrigan, in fact, who pulled the chocks away from the wheels when Lindbergh took off from San Diego on his flight to New York in 1927.

Mr. Corrigan, who had speculated openly with friends about making an unauthorized trans-Atlantic flight, flew his plane to New York on July 10, 1938, setting a solo nonstop record of 27 hours, 50 minutes for the 2,700-mile flight.

When he took off a week later, ostensibly to return to California after accepting his failure to win permission for a trans-Atlantic flight, he carried a few chocolate bars, two boxes of fig crackers and a quart of water.

Within months of his feat he had made a triumphant American tour, endorsed wrong-way products like a watch that ran backward and signed lucrative contracts for an autobiography and a movie, "The Flying Irishman," in which he played himself.

He was a test pilot during World War II and later operated an air freight service. In the 1950's, he bought an orange grove in Santa Ana, Calif., but was forced to sell most of it in the 1960's. His wife, Elizabeth, died in 1966.

After a son was killed in a plane crash on Catalina Island in 1972 he became increasingly reclusive, until 1988 when he was lured back into the limelight by an offer to display his plane at an air show.

Mr. Corrigan, who had taken it apart in 1940 and stored it in his garage, was so enthusiastic that the show's organizers became alarmed.

Although Mr. Corrigan had not flown since 1972, the organizers found it prudent to station guards on the plane's wings during his appearance at the exhibition and even discussed anchoring the tail of the plane by rope to a police car.

He is survived by two sons, Douglas, of Santa Ana, and Harry, of Apex, N.C., and a sister, Evelyn, of Santa Ynez, Calif.

December 14, 1995

Anton Rosenberg,

a Hipster Ideal, Dies at 71

Anton Rosenberg, a storied sometime artist and occasional musician who embodied the Greenwich Village hipster ideal of 1950's cool to such a laid-back degree and with such determined detachment that he never amounted to much of anything, died on Feb. 14 at a hospital near his home in Woodstock, N.Y. He was 71 and best known as the model for the character Julian Alexander in Jack Kerouac's novel "The Subterraneans."

The cause was cancer, his family said.

He was a painter of acknowledged talent, and he played the piano with such finesse that he jammed with Charlie Parker, Zoot Sims and other jazz luminaries of the day.

But if Mr. Rosenberg never made a name for himself in either art or music—or pushed himself to try—there was a reason: once he had been viewed in his hipster glory, leaning languidly against a car parked in front of Fugazzi's bar on the Avenue of the Americas, there was simply nothing more he could do to enhance his reputation.

For as Kerouac recognized, Mr. Rosenberg in his 20's, a thin, unshaven, quiet and strange young man of such dark good looks that he was frequently likened to the French actor Gerard Philipe, was the epitome of hip, an extreme esthetic that shunned enthusiasm, scorned ambition and ridiculed achievement.

It was Kerouac's friend Allen Ginsberg who discovered Fugazzi's and its coterie of hipsters of such bedrock cool that he dubbed them the subterraneans, a term Kerouac adopted as the title of his book published in 1958.

Like other Kerouac works, the book, which was written in

1953, is the most thinly disguised of fictions, one whose most strik-
ing deception was shifting its locale from New York to San Francisco to protect the publisher from any libel action by the very real
Greenwich Village regulars who populated its pages under ficti-
tious names. To Kerouac, they were cynosures of cool.

"They are hip without being slick," he wrote. "They are intel-
ligent without being corny, they are intellectual as hell and know
all about Pound without being pretentious or talking too much
about it, they are very quiet, they are very Christlike."

As for Mr. Rosenberg, or Julian Alexander, as he was called, he
was "the angel of the subterraneans," a loving man of compelling
gentleness, or as Kerouac put it: "Julian Alexander certainly is
Christlike."

By the time he made the Greenwich Village scene, Mr. Rosenberg, a native of Brooklyn whose father was a wealthy industrial-
ist, had served a year in the Army, studied briefly at the University
of North Carolina and spent a year in Paris, ostensibly studying art
on the G.I. Bill but in reality soaking up the Left Bank bohemian
atmosphere and haunting the Cafe Flore and the Cafe Deux

Magots with James Baldwin, Terry Southern and other incipient icons of American cool.

Back in New York by 1950, Mr. Rosenberg opened a print shop on Christopher Street and plunged into the hip world centered on the San Remo at Bleecker and Macdougal Streets.

He lived for a while in the East 11th Street tenement Ginsberg called Paradise Valley and had such an instinct for future chic that he was one of the first artists to move to an industrial loft in a bleak neighborhood below Canal Street years before it became the fashionable TriBeCa.

In a different life, Mr. Rosenberg might have used the loft to turn out masterpieces. But as an ultimate hipster he had other priorities, which became apparent one famous Halloween night when the crew, alerted to a shipment from the Exotic Plant Company of Laredo, Tex., peeled off from the San Remo and congregated in the loft for an all-night peyote party–cum–jam session.

Drugs, of course, were more than an accoutrement of hip. They were its very essence. And while marijuana, then an exotic drug used only by jazz musicians, was universal among the stoned cool hipsters, it was heroin that set the subterraneans apart.

Mr. Rosenberg, who appears as a character in William Burroughs's book "Junkie," was an addict for most of his adult life, which might help explain why he never made a name for himself in art or music or held a regular job after his print shop failed in the 1960's.

Fortunately, Mr. Rosenberg, whose survivors include his wife, Joan, and a brother, Ross, of Orlando, Fla., had the foresight to marry a schoolteacher so enamored of his charming, creative ways that she cheerfully supported the family while Mr. Rosenberg continued to paint, play music, amuse his friends and family. He also served as a surprisingly effective role model for his three sons: Shaun, a Manhattan restaurateur who owns Orson's on Second Avenue, Matthew, a computer consultant from the Bronx, and Jeremy, of Manhattan, a New York City police detective who specializes in drug enforcement.

February 22, 1998

EDWARD LOWE,

CAT OWNERS' BEST FRIEND

Edward Lowe, whose accidental discovery of a product he called Kitty Litter made cats more welcome household company and created a half-billion-dollar industry, died at a hospital in Sarasota, Fla.. He was 75 and had divided his time between homes in Arcadia, Fla., and Cassopolis, Mich. His son, Tom, said the cause was complications from surgery for cerebral hemorrhage.

Cats have been domesticated since ancient Egypt, but until a fateful January day in 1947, those who kept them indoors full-time paid a heavy price. For all their vaunted obsession with paw-licking cleanliness, cats, whose constitutions were adapted for arid desert climes, make such an efficient use of water that they produce a highly concentrated urine that is one of the most noxious effluences of the animal kingdom. Boxes filled with sand, sawdust or wood shavings provided a measure of relief from the resulting stench, but not enough to make cats particularly welcome in discriminating homes.

In a story he always relished telling, that began to change in 1947, when Mr. Lowe, a twenty-seven-year-old Navy veteran who had been working in his father's sawdust business, received a visit from a cat-loving Cassopolis neighbor named Kaye Draper, whose sandbox had frozen. She asked Mr. Lowe for some sawdust, but on a sudden inspiration he suggested she try something he had in the trunk of his car, a bag of kiln-dried granulated clay, a highly absorbent mineral that his father, who sold sawdust to factories to sop up grease spills, had begun offering as a fireproof alternative.

When Ms. Draper came back a few days later asking for more,

Mr. Lowe thought he might be on to something. To find out for sure, he took ten sacks, carefully wrote the words "Kitty Litter" on the sides and filled them each with five pounds of the granules. When his suggestion that they be sold at a local store to cat owners for sixty-five cents—at a time when sand was selling at a penny a pound—drew a hoot, Mr. Lowe suggested they be given away. When the customers returned asking for "Kitty Litter" by name, a business and a brand were born.

It took a while, but Mr. Lowe, who began by filling his '43 Chevy coupe with hand-filled bags of Kitty Litter and visiting pet stores and cat shows, soon had a booming business.

Adapting clay for use as a cat box litter made Mr. Lowe a millionaire many times over, in part because it has been credited with giving dogs a rival in American homes. Indeed, in 1985 cats passed dogs as the most popular American pets, and according to a survey by the Pet Industry Advisory Council, in 1994 there were 54.2 million pet dogs in the country and 63 million cats, enough to consume $600 million to $700 million worth of clay-based cat box litter, perhaps a third of it Kitty Litter and subsidiary brands created by Mr. Lowe.

He spent lavishly on research to maintain his market position in the highly competitive industry he had created. But Mr. Lowe, who recalled growing up so poor his family burned corncobs for heat and had no indoor toilet, spent even more lavishly as a conspicuous consumer, acquiring among other things, twenty-two homes, a seventy-two-foot yacht, a stable of quarter horses, a private railroad, and an entire Michigan town.

Material success had its personal price, however, as became evident in 1984, when Mr. Lowe dismissed his four children and his three sons-in-law from their company positions, saying they were conspiring to take over the company by having him declared incompetent as an alcoholic. Mr. Lowe, who denied he had a serious drinking problem, said his three daughters had joined Al-Anon, an organization for children of alcoholics, as a ruse. The daughters said they were simply trying to understand what they regarded as his strange behavior.

In part to help other entrepreneurs avoid similar family problems, Mr. Lowe created the Edward Lowe Foundation, which sponsors a variety of programs at his 3,000-acre estate in south-western Michigan. He sold his Kitty Litter operation for $200 million plus stock in 1990. It is now part of the Ralston Purina Company. And after a long, bitter estrangement, Mr. Lowe softened his views toward his family in his last few years, his son said.

In addition to his son, Tom, of Granger, Ind., Mr. Lowe, who was divorced in 1974, is survived by his second wife, Darlene; three daughters, Marilyn Miller of South Bend, Ind., Kathy Petersen of Washington, D.C., and Marcia O'Neil of Naples, Fla.; a sister, Meredith Murray of Fort Myers, Fla., and 12 grandchildren.

October 6, 1995

Maurice Sagoff, 88,

a Master of Terse Verses

on Literature

Maurice Sagoff, a reformed journalist who made a late-life name for himself abbreviating great literature into terse humorous verse, died on March 18 at a hospital near his home in Acton, Mass. He was 88 and the author of "Shrinklits: 70 of the World's Towering Classics Cut Down to Size."

At first blush it might not seem all that obvious that, say, "Crime and Punishment" required reduction to 10 couplets, even (or especially) these:

> Up-tight student
> Axes pair.
> Fearful, with the
> Cops aware.
> Yet vainglorious,
> He won't chicken
> Till by saintly
> Sonia stricken;
> Then confession,
> Trial and sentence:
> Eight Siberian years.
> Repentance
> Floods his spirit,
> Hang-ups cease,
> She will join him
> Seeking peace . . .

In that bleak
Siberian hovel,
Watch him, Sonia,
With that shovel.

Indeed, even Mr. Sagoff had long been content with the Dostoyevsky version. Then he read about a Middle Western university that had appropriated $2 million for a gymnasium and $20,000 for library books, and it set him to thinking, for Mr. Sagoff a process that frequently veered into the absurd, in this case producing the notion that with library space clearly at a premium, what the world needed was a one-inch shelf of great literature.

Mr. Sagoff shared his view in a tongue-in-cheek 1968 article for Mademoiselle magazine, which included an abbreviated "Alice in Wonderland" ("Holed up / With bunny, / Pre-teen / Acts funny / Aberrations- / Hallucinations- / Wild Scenes / Tarts, Queens / Clearly, she / Needs therapy").

For Mr. Sagoff, who for years had been dashing off doggerel to celebrate special occasions, the subversive excursion into mock literature might mercifully have ended there if the verse had not caught the eye and tickled the fancy of Elizabeth Charlotte, a New York book editor.

As Ms. Charlotte recalled, she wondered if Mr. Sagoff had enough similar verses to justify a book, called him and reached his wife, who assured the editor that her husband had composed dozens of shrinklits.

It was not until after she had commissioned a book that the editor discovered that Mr. Sagoff had no such supply but had been spurred by her interest to churn them out.

First published by Doubleday in 1970, the book was an immediate sensation, making the New York Times best-seller list and eventually becoming a staple for Workman Publishing Company, which issued a version in 1980 including modern classics like "Portnoy's Complaint" ("Alec Portnoy, none too choosy, / Went for any willing floozy; / Still a jerk in matters phallic / Alec also went for Alec . . .").

By the time "Shrinklits," his only book, was published, Mr. Sagoff, a native of Cambridge, Mass., had graduated from Boston

College, spent one happy decade working as a research librarian for the Boston Public Library system and two miserable decades working as regional editor for Fairchild Publications.

Gratefully taking early retirement in 1954, he was contentedly managing the visitor center at the Boston Children's Museum when he came up with the idea for shrinklits.

The success of the book, which has sold more than 150,000 copies and is still in print, spurred him to sell his verse to a variety of publications, including The New York Times.

He had recently finished a volume of Clerihews, a rarefied and not especially celebrated form of verse whose four lines always begin with a name, a format that allowed Mr. Sagoff to continue his interest in literature ("Oscar Wilde / Married, and fathered a child, / Which proves, you might say, / He was not toujours gai"), while expanding his humorous horizons to fields like painting ("Michelangelo Buonarroti/Carried his own personal potty/High up in the Sistine/To keep it pristine") and anthropology ("Pithecanthropus, said Mrs. Erectus,/Your friends, the big apes, may reject us,/But I think it's time you began/To stand up and act like a man"). For reasons that might seem all too obvious, he had planned to have it published privately.

Mr. Sagoff, whose first wife died in 1969, is survived by his second wife, Charlotte; two children, Sara Mitter of Montpellier, France, and Mark, of Bethesda, Md., and four grandchildren.

March 29, 1998

CORRECTION: An obituary on March 29 about Maurice Sagoff, a writer of terse humorous verses, misspelled the names of the New York editor who commissioned his book, "Shrinklits." She is Elisabeth Scharlatt, not Elizabeth Charlotte.

Robert Saudek Is Dead at 85,

a Pioneer of Culture on TV

Robert Saudek, who gave the era of live television some of its most elevating and electrifying moments as the creator of the acclaimed "Omnibus" series of eclectic cultural programs, died on Thursday at a hospital in Baltimore. He was 85 and lived in Washington.

Having served as alchemist in chief of what is often recalled as the golden age of television, Mr. Saudek went on to help keep the luster of the 1950's alive, first as the founding president of the Museum of Broadcasting and later as the head of the division for motion pictures, broadcasting and recorded sound of the Library of Congress.

By the time the Ford Foundation asked him to direct its experimental TV/Radio Workshop in 1951, Mr. Saudek, then a Harvard-educated ABC vice president, had established himself as an innovative network executive specializing in high-minded radio documentaries. These illuminated issues like the Marshall Plan, urban slums, public education and American Communism.

It is not exactly clear what the foundation had in mind when it put him in charge of the workshop and gave him his head, but what it got was "Omnibus," an often daring 90-minute weekly celebration of Mr. Saudek's wide-ranging interests and his determination to share his enthusiasm for music, art, theater and fun with the masses.

After all, as a child in Pittsburgh, where his father was an orchestra conductor and his mother a symphony violinist, Mr. Saudek, who sang in the Harvard Glee Club, grew up with a love of great music. He saw no reason why it or other arts should be reserved for a cultural elite.

As a producer in an entertainment medium whose mass-market appeal had been defined by Milton Berle's wearing a dress, Mr. Saudek knew what he was up against. But he also knew how to use the leverage of celebrity and sheer talent to make a cultural point.

Yes, he once had Jose Limon dance "The Moor's Pavanne," but his idea for a segment on dance as a man's game was not to show men in tights. It was to get Mickey Mantle, Johnny Unitas and Sugar Ray Robinson to demonstrate their famous athletic motions while Gene Kelly translated them into dance. And when Mr. Saudek presented "Oedipus Rex," he had the "Omnibus" host, Alistair Cooke, prime his viewers by pointing out that more people would see that single Sunday performance than the cumulative total of all the people who had seen all the previous productions over 2,500 years.

Not all his programs won raves. Some purists, for example, were aghast when he presented a radically abbreviated, 90-minute version of "King Lear," but that was Orson Welles in the title role.

As television's first great impresario, Mr. Saudek gave Leonard Bernstein his first star turn (expounding on Beethoven's Fifth, with the opening bars painted right on the studio floor) and introduced Jacques Cousteau to the world of television. He also gave television viewers their first looks at Agnes de Mille, Leopold Stokowski, Peter Ustinov (as Dr. Samuel Johnson), Mike Nichols and Elaine May, Pablo Casals, Artur Rubinstein, Marian Anderson, Isaac Stern, Yehudi Menuhin, Igor Stravinsky, Glenn Gould, Danny Kaye, Yo-Yo Ma and Dr. Seuss.

In an age of pioneering television, "Omnibus," which went on the air in 1952, operated so far beyond the frontiers of conventional programming that it was passed like a hot potato among the three networks. And except for a season or two, it was considered too advanced for prime time but was relegated to the culture gulch of late Sunday afternoons. There it proved so addictive that it disrupted dinner schedules in every time zone.

No wonder. He cast his imaginative net so wide it was hard to tell what Mr. Saudek would dream up next. Over its eight seasons, regular viewers might see a demonstration of a new X-ray film one week, a witch-doctor dance another week and in between an original play by William Saroyan, an essay on Maine lobstermen by E. B. White, an S. J. Perelman look at Hollywood, and Bert Lahr in George Bernard Shaw's "Androcles and the Lion."

After the Ford Foundation withdrew its support in 1957, on the assumption that "Omnibus" had established itself and could go it alone, Mr. Saudek formed his own production company, which kept it alive until 1961. Then it finally sank beneath the waves of a network demand for programs that appealed to the widest possible audience.

Before accepting William S. Paley's commission to establish the Museum of Broadcasting (now the Museum of Television and Radio) in 1974, Mr. Saudek produced other acclaimed programs, including "Profiles in Courage," "Leonard Bernstein and the New York Philharmonic" and "S. Hurok Presents." He won 11 Emmys and 7 Peabody Awards.

A small, wiry man ("a dime among nickels," as he put it), Mr. Saudek had an aversion to pomposity and such a penchant for wit that when he and the New Yorker writer John Bainbridge got together swapping knee-slappers, their peals of laughter would draw a crowd.

When Mr. Saudek's children went through his files after his death, they were not surprised to find that their father, who had been singing "Guys and Dolls" in his hospital room a few days earlier, had a folder labeled "Fun." It included a full-page Library of Congress memo on how to use a telephone hold button.

Mr. Saudek is survived by his wife, Elizabeth; four sons, Richard of Montpelier, Vt., Christopher of Lutherville, Md., Robert of Atlanta and Stephen of Lexington, Mass.; a daughter, Mary Elizabeth Jaffee of Lexington; 14 grandchildren and a great-grandchild.

March 17, 1997

FRED ROSENSTIEL, 83,

DEVOTED HIS LIFE TO PLANTING FLOWERS

Fred Rosenstiel, who spent his life planting gardens to brighten the lives of his fellow New Yorkers, and to alleviate an abiding sadness in his heart, died on Tuesday at the Western Queens Community Hospital in Astoria. He was 83 and lived recently in Astoria.

In a city where corps of volunteer gardeners seem to spring up like wildflowers, Mr. Rosenstiel was a volunteer gardener with a difference, a man so driven that for four decades he did little else.

Since arriving in New York in 1951, Mr. Rosenstiel, the son of a prosperous Dutch businessman who left him enough money to live on, had made gardens, coaxing green shoots of life from the New York soil.

"He was a master plantsman," said Barbara Earnest, the director of the New York Horticultural Society, recalling Mr. Rosenstiel as the city's most dedicated and prolific volunteer gardener, one who lent his expertise and his brawn to community gardening groups and worked on his own to plant flowers on virtually any patch of unpaved earth in the city.

Whether part of a group or working alone, Mr. Rosenstiel, whose name means "rose stalk" in German, planted gardens in parks, vacant lots, schools, housing projects, hospitals and homeless shelters.

A founder of the Green Guerillas, a group that has organized and tended hundreds of community gardens since 1973, he was also an unpaid consultant to the New York City Council on the Environment and to many other organizations.

A longtime resident of the Upper West Side, he would leave his apartment on West 113th Street at 8 A.M. and would rarely be home before midnight, sometimes visiting three or more community gardens in a day.

When he was not on his knees, digging his hands into the earth to root out Japanese knotweed threatening a garden in Riverside Park or planting the yellow flowering lamium he knew would thrive in the ubiquitous New York shade, Mr. Rosenstiel, a tall, powerfully built man with granite features, could often be found immersed in a newspaper at a Broadway coffee shop.

Known as a sad man who found an elusive joy in gardening and music, Mr. Rosenstiel became a familiar figure on the Upper West Side, a neighborhood character in a beret and tweed jacket who carried a shopping bag crammed with gardening equipment and made it a point of honor never to travel anywhere except by subway.

He often held court at the old Mill Luncheonette at 111th Street and Broadway, where he would harangue Columbia University students, often urging them to adopt surprisingly radical positions.

They called him "the Professor."

"Perhaps I would have had a more interesting career had I been forced to make a living," he once told a friend, before adding, "These are the ironies of life."

Mr. Rosenstiel was on intimate terms with such ironies. In his family the ironies twisted back on themselves.

His parents were German Jews who immigrated to England, where they suffered such anti-German prejudice during World War I that they moved to the Netherlands.

Mr. Rosenstiel, who was born in London and grew up there and in Rotterdam before going to school in Switzerland, was the only member of his family who survived the Nazis.

His only brother was killed fighting as a soldier with the Dutch Army. His parents and several aunts, uncles and cousins died at Auschwitz.

Mr. Rosenstiel, who was in England at the outbreak of the war and who later served four years as a seaman with the Britain-based

Dutch Navy, seemed to find it hard to forgive himself for surviving the Holocaust, friends said. He felt such guilt, he once told a friend, that he felt he was not entitled to any happiness.

That, he explained, is why he never married, never pursued a career. He simply planted gardens, a delight he had stumbled on at a cooperative London youth hostel when he volunteered to tend its garden as a way of getting out of doing the dishes.

In his later years he found a measure of comfort with Esther Lazarson, a woman who had loved him since the day they met in 1969 and who took him in when he became too sick to care for himself four years ago.

Ms. Lazarson, a native of England who has lived in New York off and on since 1951, recalled yesterday that Mr. Rosenstiel had once offered her a white begonia if she would stay in New York, but she wanted more than he was prepared to give at the time. He had learned from the Holocaust, she said, how much you can lose and how quickly when you love too much.

"He gave me a white begonia when I came back," she added.

June 16, 1995

Sydney Guilaroff, 89,
Stylist to Stars, Is Dead

Sydney Guilaroff, who gave Claudette Colbert her bangs, made Lucille Ball a redhead, gave Judy Garland her "Wizard of Oz" braids and cut, curled, coiffed and cosseted virtually every other MGM star in a 40-year reign as Hollywood's most creative and celebrated hairdresser, died on Wednesday at a nursing home in Beverly Hills, Calif. He was 89.

His son Jon said the cause was pneumonia.

Movie stars had hair before Mr. Guilaroff came along, and there were presumably studio hairdressers, too.

But there was a reason that he was the first to receive screen credits and a reason that Greta Garbo, Greer Garson, Elizabeth Taylor, Joan Crawford, Norma Shearer, Hedy Lamarr, Ava Gardner, Lana Turner, Lena Horne, Grace Kelly, Debbie Reynolds, Kathryn Grayson, Ann-Margret, Marilyn Monroe and myriad other stars would not dream of making a movie—or sometimes a move—without Mr. Guilaroff.

He was at once a master craftsman—a wizard with scissors—and an acknowledged artist, one with such an instinctive eye for the possibilities of beauty that he could look at a face and instantly see it transformed—by a curl, a flip, a wave, a daring cut or a bit of color.

As the chief stylist at Metro-Goldwyn-Mayer during the studio's golden years from 1934 to the late 1970's, he was the man behind the hairdos in more than a thousand movies.

Among them were "Ben-Hur," "Quo Vadis," "Camille," "The Philadelphia Story," "Some Like It Hot," "Gentlemen Prefer Blondes," and what he called his greatest challenge, the 1938 production of "Marie Antoinette," which required 2,000 court wigs (some with actual birds in cages), lesser wigs for 3,000 extras and Norma Shearer's monumental bejeweled and feathered artists' ball creation.

A man with an enormous talent for friendship who both gave and inspired loyalty, Mr. Guilaroff (pronounced GIL-er-ahf) not only did actresses' hair; by his own account he shared their private moments of triumph and disaster: the man Grace Kelly summoned to Monaco to style her hair for her wedding to Prince Ranier; the man who sat with the bedridden Joan Crawford the night she won an Oscar for "Mildred Pierce"; the "surrogate father" to whom Elizabeth Taylor turned for comfort when her husband Mike Todd was killed in a plane crash and the friend a distraught Marilyn Monroe called the night she died in August 1962.

Along the way, Mr. Guilaroff heard so many secrets it was all he could do to hold them in until he disgorged them in his memoirs, "Crowning Glories," an as-told-to tell-all told to Cathy Griffin and published by General Publishing Group last year.

Well, maybe he did not tell all the all, but his accounts of his long-term affairs with Greta Garbo and Ava Gardner should be enough to establish Mr. Guilaroff as one of Hollywood's great lovers, even if neither actress is around to verify the details.

Even before Miss Colbert discovered the 21-year-old "Mr. Sydney" in 1928 at Antoine's, the elegant Saks Fifth Avenue salon in Manhattan, and walked out with the bangs and bob that would be her trademark for the rest of her life, Mr. Guilaroff had inadvertently changed the shape of women's hair and made his mark on the movies.

Five years earlier, when he was a 16-year-old apprentice stylist at the old McAlpin Hotel in New York City, as he later recalled it, he created a national hairstyle rage known as the "shingle" for a walk-in client he did not realize at the time was the silent screen star Louise Brooks.

For all his natural talent and later acclaim, Mr. Guilaroff became a hairdresser by accident. A native of London who grew up in Canada, first in Winnipeg, Manitoba, and later in Montreal, he had a decidedly artistic bent as a child and a flair for playing the piano and for painting. But he dreamed of becoming an architect before a family financial squeeze led him to leave home at 13 and seek employment in New York.

So poor that he sometimes slept on park benches, he held a series of menial jobs before he landed at the McAlpin salon as a handyman, picking up his trade almost by osmosis and proving so adept that by the time he was 17 he was at Antoine's. Within a few years, he had his own salon at Bonwit Teller.

Miss Colbert's raves made him a favorite in the New York theater world, and drew such clients as Libby Holman, Ginger Rogers and Clare Boothe Luce. But it was Miss Crawford's insistence on coming to New York for a Guilaroff styling before every picture that led Louis B. Mayer to take him to Hollywood in 1934.

A favorite of directors as well as actors, Mr. Guilaroff was tapped for two appearances on the screen, once in person as Geraldine Page's hairdresser in "Sweet Bird of Youth," and once by inference when "Blackie's," the name of the salon that is the setting of Clare Boothe Luce's play "The Women," "which was based on an actual incident involving a former Guilaroff client, was changed to "Sydney's" for the movie version.

Although Mr. Guilaroff's movie clients included virtually all the major male stars of the era, women were clearly his forte.

Despite all his love of women, and theirs for him, he never married. Yet, as the sixth of seven children, including five older sisters, he longed for family life and saw no reason that his single status should keep him from being a father.

So in 1938, at the age of 31, the man who had revolutionized the nation's hairstyles blithely made legal history by becoming the first never-married man in the United States who was allowed to adopt a child, a year-old son he named Jon, after Joan Crawford. Three years later, he adopted a second son, named Eugene for Mr. Guilaroff's father.

As Jon recalled it, Mr. Guilaroff was a doting father who made it a point to have dinner with his sons every night and who provided them a special childhood bonus: Hollywood's greatest stylist gave them haircuts.

Besides Jon, of Santa Monica, Calif., and Eugene, of Alvagon, Ky., Mr. Guilaroff is survived by two sisters, Rita Loadman of Winnipeg and Eva Feldman of Montreal.

June 1, 1997

Emil Sitka,

Favorite Foil of Three Stooges,

Dies at 83

Emil Sitka, a character actor who portrayed butlers and others with such exquisite dignity and in such rarefied company it was inevitable that if he didn't get poked in the eye or bopped on the head he was sure to catch a cream pie in the kisser, died on Jan. 16 at a hospital near his home in Camarillo, Calif. He was 83 and had been a favorite foil of the Three Stooges.

Since the death of the last of the Stooges, Joe DeRita, in 1993, Mr. Sitka had been widely regarded by the Stooges' dedicated fans as the last living link to a madcap, slapstick era that to virtually everyone else's dismay shows no signs of going away.

Whether he was playing a butler, a businessman, a society figure or a mad scientist, with the Three Stooges on the loose, before the 20-minute short had run its manic, two-reel course, Mr. Sitka could be counted on to suffer at least one indignity, sometimes several.

For although he appeared in only 35 of the 190 Stooges shorts made by Columbia Pictures from 1934 to 1958, Mr. Sitka, a tall, slender man with a quavering voice, once estimated that he had portrayed 70 different characters, sometimes four in a single picture.

If he wasn't being attacked directly by one of the Stooges, Mr. Sitka, who also appeared in five of the Stooges' six feature films, was always susceptible to mechanical menace. As he once recalled it, he would be the actor with a tube up his sleeve who would pick up a phone and get a face full of water.

Such sight gags coupled with his precise comic timing and the surprising nuance he brought to his roles helped make Mr. Sitka a favorite among the Stoogies, as the group's fans are known.

Mr. Sitka, who was born in Johnstown, Pa., and orphaned at 12, got his first taste of acting as a teenager in church passion plays while living with a priest in Pittsburgh. But it was only after a rails-riding hobo period in the Depression that he made his way to Los Angeles in 1936 and found a home in the theater, literally.

He lived in the dressing room of a small theater for two years while taking small parts and eventually graduating to directing.

Recruited by a scout for Columbia in 1946, Mr. Sitka became a fixture in the comedy shorts the studio was grinding out by the mile.

Mr. Sitka later said he appeared in 450 movies, but for all his other work, including bit parts in a number of feature films, it was his roles with the Stooges that assured him apparently permanent fame through the seemingly endless television showings of the Three Stooges.

Making his Stooges debut in "Halfwits Holiday," Mr. Sitka joined the troupe just in time to claim the distinction of appear-

(Ventura County Star)

ing with each of the six men who portrayed Stooges over the years: Moe Howard, his brothers Shemp and Curly (Jerome), Larry Fine, Joe Besser and Joe DeRita.

The movie, released in 1947, was the last major appearance by Curly, who had a stroke during production. He was replaced by Shemp, who had been a member of the Stooges' original vaudeville troupe.

For all the varied characters Mr. Sitka portrayed, his most memorable role was as a harried justice of the peace in the 1947 short "Brideless Groom," in which Shemp, who is to inherit a fortune if he marries within 24 hours, is besieged by so many fortune-hunting prospective brides that a free-for-all erupts every time Mr. Sitka tries to begin the service with the words, "Hold hands, you lovebirds."

The line became so famous that Mr. Sitka, who was forever being asked to inscribe the words on wedding photographs, would sometimes be called during a Stoogie wedding service and asked to intone the words over the phone.

The man who proudly drove a car with the license plate "STOOGES" always obliged.

After all, on paper at least, he was one of the Three Stooges. In 1974, Mr. Sitka signed a contract to replace the ailing Larry Fine in a planned Stooges feature, but with the death of Moe Howard the next year, the film was never made.

If the Three Stooges are a decidedly specialized taste, they have a way of insinuating themselves into mainstream movies.

In Quentin Tarantino's 1994 hit, "Pulp Fiction," for example, Mr. Sitka's voice can be heard from an off-camera television set as he yet once again says the magic words: "Hold hands, you lovebirds."

Mr. Sitka, who regarded naming children a creative exercise, is survived by two daughters, Eelonka Klugman of Simi Valley, Calif., and Little-Star Martotella of Victorville, Calif.; four sons, all of California, Rudigor of Lawndale, Storm of Anaheim, Darrow of Hesperia, and Saxon of Camarillo; 13 grandchildren and 4 great-grandchildren.

January 25, 1998

FRED FELDMAN,

HELICOPTER REPORTER,

DIES AT 63

Fred Feldman, New York radio's first helicopter reporter who spent 16 airborne years monitoring traffic for rush-hour commuters and who invented the term "rubbernecking delays" to explain why they would be late for work, died on Friday at his home in Roseland, N.J. He was 63.

The cause was a heart attack, according to his sister, Joann Fessler. She said her brother, who had stopped flying after suffering a heart attack and undergoing bypass surgery in 1978, had been scheduled for further bypass surgery this week.

Although he had a long and distinguished later career, including seven years as director of the Shadow Traffic reporting service and eight as communications director for the Department of Transportation, Mr. Feldman was best known for the years he spent flying Helicopter 710 over the city's often-clogged highways and providing regular traffic updates for station WOR-AM.

At a time when the venerable talk station's vast and fanatically loyal audience regarded regulars like John A. Gambling, Ed and Pegeen Fitzgerald and Alfred and Dora McCann as intimate members of their own families, Mr. Feldman was a beloved member of the family almost from the moment he took to the air in April 1962.

Promptly dubbed Fearless Fred, by Mr. Gambling, Mr. Feldman was such a hit and had such an engaging personality that within months the 29-year-old bachelor was receiving mash notes by the hundreds.

Only the second helicopter pilot to provide radio traffic reports (Francis Gary Powers, the U-2 pilot shot down over the Soviet Union in 1960, had been the first, for a Los Angeles station), Mr. Feldman was the first to emerge as a significant radio personality, and, in his case, something of a local institution.

He is generally given credit for being the first person to have recognized that when things went dark on Nov. 9, 1965, it was not an isolated power failure but a vast blackout, which turned out to extend over the entire Northeast.

Mr. Feldman was a pharmacist's son who was born in Manhattan and grew up in Forest Hills, Queens, and Washington Heights. He developed such an early and intense interest in flying that by the time he attended the University of Connecticut he had built so many model airplanes that his roommate complained that if he hung one more model from the ceiling the entire dorm room would take off.

Mr. Feldman, who spent seven years in the Air Force, flying jets and serving as a flying instructor, became a radio reporter by accident. While working for a commercial helicopter service, he was engaged by WOR to ferry a reporter around the city during the morning rush hour, but when Mr. Feldman showed up the station had not yet hired a reporter and he was sent up on his own.

Although he had no radio training and no knowledge of traffic flows, Mr. Feldman, who soon became a station employee, quickly learned the ropes. Balancing a clipboard on his knee while usually using both hands to fly, he delivered crisp reports every 10 minutes or so, learning the vagaries of traffic patterns as he went along and developing compelling lingo on the fly. The L.I.E., he quickly concluded, was "a big lie," not an expressway at all but "the world's longest parking lot."

As for the ubiquitous delays, Mr. Feldman was amazed to discover phantom bottlenecks, which he termed rubbernecking delays caused by motorists slowing down to gawk at some accident or other roadside distraction. (A couple necking in Riverside Park, he once reported, caused a four-mile backup on the West Side Highway.)

After his 1978 heart attack, Mr. Feldman concentrated on

desk jobs, retiring last year after two years as director of special projects for the Transcom consortium of regional traffic agencies. His sister of Ramsey, N.J., is his only immediate survivor.

October 20, 1996

Frank Kurtz, 85,
World War II Hero, Dies

Frank Kurtz, who ran away from home at 12, set aviation speed records as a teenager, became an Olympic high diver in the 1930's and then won fame as a pilot in World War II, died on Oct. 31 at his home in Toluca Lake, Calif. He was 85.

His wife, Margo, said the cause was the effects of a head injury suffered in a fall a year ago.

Mr. Kurtz, a career Air Force officer who later worked as an executive with the William May Garland development company in Los Angeles, is also survived by his daughter, Swoosie Kurtz, who is surely the only actress named for an airplane.

The plane was called the Swoose, after a Kay Kaiser song about Alexander the Swoose, a creature that was half swan and half goose, and like its namesake it was a hybrid affair, cobbled together in Australia early in the war from the parts of several battered B-17's that had somehow survived the Japanese attack on Clark Field in the Philippines hours after Pearl Harbor.

With Capt. Frank Kurtz at the controls, the Swoose quickly became famous, flying hundreds of missions, surviving forced landings and repeated attacks by Japanese fighters and making headlines on the home front, including the time when Captain Kurtz, ferrying a contingent of generals and visiting Congressmen, had to make a scary forced landing in the Australian bush as a crewman forcibly restrained a hysterical Representative Lyndon B. Johnson.

At a time when the United States was desperately short of heroes, Captain Kurtz was the genuine article.

A native of Davenport, Iowa, he grew up in Kansas City, Mo., a decidedly independent child who began making legends early.

There was the time, for example, when he went to a local swimming pool, tugged on the lifeguard's trunks and said: "I don't know how to swim, Mister, but I want to dive off of that board. Will you catch me?" Then, as the lifeguard obliged, the little boy made his first dive and discovered a vocation.

By the time stepfather problems prompted him to leave home for good at the age of 12, he was haunting the pool at the Kansas City Athletic Club, where, in a pattern that would be repeated throughout his life, his charm, his good cheer and his sense of adventure earned him a ready welcome.

"He never lacked for a meal or a bed," his wife recalled the other day. "People liked having him around so much he could always find someone to take him in."

Like a lot of boys, including some other runaways, he hawked newspapers, in his case with such élan that he was hailed in the newspaper he sold as the best-dressed and most polite newsboy in Kansas City.

During an exhibition at the club, Johnny Weissmuller, the 1924 and 1928 Olympic swimming champion, saw him dive, recognized his promise and told him that if he wanted to make the Olympics he would need a skilled coach, like Clyde Swendsen, a storied figure at the old Hollywood Athletic Club.

Taking the advice to heart, the youth hitchhiked to Los Angeles, sought out the coach, impressed him and was soon as much a favorite among the directors, producers and studio executives at the Hollywood club as he had been with the businessmen in Kansas City. As he honed his diving and made his way through Hollywood High School and later the University of Southern California, they virtually adopted him.

When Frank Bireley, the orange-drink magnate, taught him to fly when he was 16, the youth had a second vocation. He was soon spending almost as much time in the air as he was in the diving pool, eventually setting half a dozen international speed records.

His hopes of making the 1932 Olympic diving team received a setback when he was told that the club, which had a pretty good older diver, did not have enough money to take him to a championship meet in Honolulu in 1931. Knowing that he would have to make a name for himself at a major meet to make the Olympic team, the ever-resourceful Mr. Kurtz talked his way aboard a Hawaii-bound tanker, spent three weeks at sea, arrived in time to help the team win the championship and was on his way to the Los Angeles Olympics.

He was a little off on some of his dives, he said later, taking the bronze, but along the way he ripped off a daring dive of such graceful perfection that he had the crowd on its feet, and his friend and fellow diver, Alan Ladd, was heard saying he wished he had the courage to try such a dive. Competing despite an injury, he failed to win a medal at the 1936 Games, but he was still good enough in 1940 to make the official Olympic team for Games that were canceled because of the war in Europe.

By then, Mr. Kurtz was an Army Air Corps officer, and when the United States entered the war the next year, he was in the thick of it from Day 1.

One of the few officers stationed at the Clark base to heed the advice to dig a foxhole in the event of an air attack, he was one of the comparative few to survive the raid, which, in one of the abiding mysteries of the war, caught America's front line of war planes, including 35 of the new B-17's, lined up wing-tip to wing-tip 10 hours after the attack on Pearl Harbor. Casualties ran to 75 percent.

Among the dead Americans whom Captain Kurtz helped stack "like so much cord wood," he told his wife, were the crewmen he had served with for four years.

After taking to the air to help in a brief, brave but ineffective defense, he made his way first to Java and then to Melbourne, Australia, where as a top aide to the Air Corps commanding general, he was a crucial figure in preparations to press the air war against Japan.

But before the Swoose was ready, Captain Kurtz participated in a footnote to later American history. Touring a publisher's mansion that would become a military headquarters in Australia, he was trailed by the owner's 10-year-old son, a little boy so enthralled with his tales of recent combat that Captain Kurtz took off his own air wings and pinned them on a future American citizen, Rupert Murdoch.

As a major, he returned to the United States a hero in August 1942, typically setting a speed record in the Swoose, helped to sell war bonds for a while, but insisted on returning to combat, if only, he said, for the opportunity to fly better aircraft than the early model B-17's, which were known as B-17D's.

Forming a unit known as the Swoose group, Colonel Kurtz, as he had become, flew 60 missions in Italy before being reassigned as the commander of Kirtland Air Force Base in Albuquerque, N.M., which provided air support for the Manhattan atomic bomb project, and where he ended the war.

Mr. Kurtz, who later became active in Olympic affairs, retired from the Air Force in 1960, but not before he had flown the Swoose on one last flight, to Washington, where the plane, the lone survivor of the nation's prewar Pacific air fleet, was installed in the Smithsonian Institution.

November 9, 1996

J. Edward Day, 82,

Postmaster Who Brought in

the ZIP Code

J. Edward Day, the wisecracking Cabinet officer who gave the nation a million laughs and the five-digit ZIP code as Postmaster General for three ebullient years, died on Tuesday in Hunt Valley, Md. He was 82 and lived in Chevy Chase, Md., 20815, as it has been known since Mr. Day inaugurated the ZIP code system on July 1, 1963.

The cause was a heart attack while Mr. Day was in Hunt Valley for a meeting, his family said.

When President-elect John F. Kennedy picked Mr. Day to be Postmaster General, Washington insiders were understandably puzzled. True, Mr. Day had been active in Democratic politics, first in his native Illinois and later in California, where he became an executive with the Prudential Insurance Company of America, but unlike most of his predecessors as Postmaster General he had not been a party chairman.

Yes, Mr. Day, a University of Chicago graduate who received a law degree from Harvard University and served on a submarine in World War II, was a protégé of Adlai Stevenson when Mr. Stevenson was Governor of Illinois, serving first as a legal and legislative assistant and later as state insurance commissioner. But given the Kennedy feelings toward Mr. Stevenson, an undeclared rival for the 1960 Presidential nomination, that was hardly a recommendation.

And yes, Mr. Day was a Kennedy delegate to the 1960 nominating convention, but only after Mr. Day's first choice, Gov. Edmund G. (Pat) Brown, had faded from contention.

If anyone doubted that Mr. Day had been picked because he had a reputation as a highly capable administrator with a quick grasp of complex issues, there was always his own explanation for how he met most of the qualifications for a top spot in the Kennedy Administration: "I went to Harvard, I served in the Navy and my wife went to Vassar."

Whatever his qualifications, as the most obscure member of the Kennedy Cabinet—and a man so unknown to official Washington that by his own account he was either ignored at high-powered cocktail parties or mistaken for somebody's security guard—the short, sandy-haired Mr. Day began making a name for himself almost as soon as he took his position behind the oversized desk in the huge Postmaster General's office, the Government's largest, "a lobby looking for a hotel" as he described it.

Within weeks he was known as the Kennedy Administration's resident wit and house raconteur, a man who claimed to have received hundreds of "by the way" letters, which began by offering congratulations and ended by asking for jobs.

Mr. Day said that when a meat association had asked for a stamp honoring the hamburger, he had told the group that "we had chewed their suggestion over and decided to put it on the back burner."

As he later recalled it, Mr. Kennedy had given him three goals: reduce the department's $1 billion deficit, improve service and raise employee morale. By most accounts he accomplished all three, slashing the deficit, streamlining mail deliveries and signing the first labor contract with the postal workers union.

By far his most far-reaching act was putting in place the ZIP (for Zoning Improvement Plan) code, an idea postal executives had been studying for years. With the assistance of Mr. ZIP, a cartoon character, Mr. Day sent notifications to every household in the country, the largest mass mailing up to that time.

Despite assurances that the system would speed deliveries and cut costs, the idea was widely denounced. Like the famous New Yorker cartoon in which the dowager tells her travel agent that if God had wanted people to fly jets he'd have had the

Wright Brothers invent them, as New York, 21, N.Y., became New York., N.Y., 10021, many Americans seemed distrustful of any system Benjamin Franklin had not personally approved.

Although ZIP codes did streamline mail delivery, the main effect was to revolutionize mass marketing by providing a quick way to pinpoint potential customers by income level.

Mr. Day resigned less than a month after the ZIP code went into effect, not because of the controversy, he said, but because he was finding it hard to get by on his $25,000 annual salary. Mr. Day, who had used his experience as Illinois insurance commissioner to become a high-paid insurance executive, reaped similar rewards when he returned to private law practice with clients that included the Advertising Mail Marketing Association.

In recent years, Mr. Day, who wrote several lighthearted books, including "My Appointed Round," had spent much of his time at his farm in Barnesville, Md., where after an abortive effort to raise yaks his stock included llamas and cows.

He is survived by his wife, Mary Louise; two daughters, Geraldine Zurn, of Erie, Pa., and Mary Louise Himmelfarb, of Oak Park, Ill.; a brother William of Sierra Vista, Ariz., and five grandchildren.

November 1, 1996

CORRECTION: An obituary on Nov. 1 about J. Edward Day, the Postmaster General who introduced the ZIP code system in 1963, misstated the history of his home ZIP code in Chevy Chase, Md. It was originally 20015; later it was changed to 20815.

Maria Reiche, 95,

Keeper of an Ancient

Peruvian Puzzle, Dies

Maria Reiche, who spent half a century as the self-appointed guardian of an obscure pre-Incan culture's most mysterious legacy—a vast, dazzling tableau of giant birds, animals, plants and intricate geometric patterns scratched into the stark desert floor— died on June 8 in a hospital in Lima, Peru. She was 95 and was known as the Lady of the Lines.

To see the lines near Nazca, in southern Peru, from the air— and there is no other way to make out the fabulous figures, some hundreds of yards across—the vast tapestry looks very much like the haphazard markings on a giant child's chalkboard.

There is a monkey with a whimsical spiral tail here, a condor there—a whale, a shark, a pelican, a spider, a hummingbird, an owl-faced man, a pair of hands, other birds and animals, flowers, and an array of geometric shapes. There is also a profusion of string-straight lines, some extending for miles, none suggesting an immediate explanation of why they were drawn.

After almost 60 years of intense, if highly speculative, scholarly scrutiny, it is hard to tell which is the greater mystery:

Why the valley-dwelling Nazcan people would decorate the surrounding desert mesas with figures so large their shapes could not even be discerned before the age of aviation 2,000 years later.

Or why an adventuresome German woman who came to South America on a whim to tutor a diplomat's children would abandon all other pursuits to devote her life to an almost obsessive preoccupation with the Nazca lines.

Whatever possessed her to make them her life's work, almost from the time she first saw them in 1941, Ms. Reiche (pronounced RYE-kuh) was the acknowledged and acclaimed curator of the Nazca lines.

Living in a small house in the desert so she could personally protect the delicate lines from careless visitors, Ms. Reiche—who became a Peruvian citizen in 1994—shooed away intruders even as an old woman in a wheelchair.

Over five decades she meticulously measured and mapped the intricate giant glyphs, swept away an accumulation of black dust to restore 1,000 of the lines to their original brilliance and used her own funds to hire guards and finance research projects.

All the while, she tried to figure out what the lines meant to the Nazcans, who carved them on a series of barren mesas covering 200 square miles of a long, narrow desert wedged between the Andes Mountains and the Pacific Ocean 250 miles south of Lima.

Whatever possessed them to scrape away the covering of fist-sized black rocks to expose the yellow-white hardpan underneath in a series of narrow trenches only a few inches deep forming an array of giant patterns, the Nazcans could hardly have wished for a more geologically stable canvas to preserve their mysterious handiwork.

The site is one of the driest spots on earth, drawing an average of only 20 minutes of rainfall a year. Because of a buffering cushion of warm air, it is virtually windless.

The result is a land so devoid of erosion that a footprint can last 1,000 years and the tracks of chariots used by warring conquistador factions in the 16th century are still visible.

The lines, which were discovered in modern times in 1926, were threatened by modern encroachments. The Pan American Highway, it was later discovered, had cut through a giant lizard in 1939. But nobody could have wished for a more dedicated or effective protector than Ms. Reiche.

A native of Dresden, Germany, who received a mathematics degree from the local university and who spoke five languages,

Ms. Reiche went to Peru as a tutor in 1932. She later became a translator in Lima and met Paul Kosok, a Long Island University scholar, who became her mentor.

Mr. Kosok, whose interest in irrigation led him to investigate whether the Nazca lines might have been irrigation ditches, quickly concluded that the shallow trenches, which range from 5 to 18 inches wide, could not have been used for irrigation. But when he happened to be standing near one of the long straight lines at sunset on June 22, 1941, he made a discovery that would change his life and changed Ms. Reiche's even more.

He noticed that the line pointed directly at the setting sun, suggesting that it was a marker for the winter solstice. Six months later, Ms. Reiche discovered a line pointing at the summer solstice, and a full-blown theory was born: that the Nazca lines formed an elaborate celestial calendar, or as Mr. Kosok put it, "the world's largest astronomy book."

Although the initial interest was on the straight lines, once Mr. Kosok had mapped the intricate path of one circuitous line and discovered that it formed a detailed image of a bird, the interest broadened.

Ms. Reiche, who took over Mr. Kosok's work in 1948 after he left Peru, quickly discovered and mapped 18 other animal glyphs and over the following decades elaborated on Mr. Kosok's calendar theory, deciding that at least some of the glyphs were representations of constellations.

The calendar theory was clearly more plausible than the one that held that the lines were part of a guidance system for prehistoric spaceships. But scholars whose various rival theories held that the lines had religious, social or even athletic significance nibbled away at the calendar idea—finding, for example, that most of the lines did not point to any celestial bodies.

But Ms. Reiche may have made a miscalculation not unlike that made by Columbus, who made his accidental discovery of the New World through a fundamental error: his belief that the earth was much smaller (and the Indies, therefore, much closer to Europe than they are). Her miscalculation may have been in her conviction that at least some of the animal figures were images of stellar constellations.

Recent scholarship by her protégée, Phyllis B. Pitluga, senior astronomer at the Adler Planetarium in Chicago, concluded that all of the animal figures are indeed representations of heavenly shapes. But she contends that they are not shapes of constellations but of what might be called counter constellations, the irregular-shaped dark patches within the twinkling expanse of the Milky Way.

Whatever the explanation, largely as a result of Ms. Reiche's work, the Nazca lines have become a major tourist attraction and were designated a world heritage site by Unesco in 1995.

And at her death, Ms. Reiche, who leaves no immediate survivors, was hailed as a national treasure. President Alberto K. Fujimori of Peru went so far as to suggest that the Nazca lines should be renamed the Reiche lines.

June 15, 1998

Walter J. Kuron,
of Red Baron Era, Dies at 102

Walter J. Kuron, a German-born choirmaster who made music his life and his World War I dogfighting days his legend, died Tuesday at a New Jersey nursing home the way he lived, listening to Bach. He was 102 and had not quite lived down the myth that he was the last man alive to have flown with Baron Manfred von Richthofen, the Red Baron.

The myth is a tribute to nostalgia for a rapidly fading era of living memory, to the lasting glow of the Red Baron's gallantry, to Mr. Kuron's own longevity—and, just possibly, to his own sense of humor.

A man who had three pianos in his house but not one scale-model Fokker, Mr. Kuron spent more than 60 years directing church choirs, playing, building and repairing church organs, performing on the piano, organizing and leading chamber-music recitals and listening to recorded music. And yet he is still remembered chiefly for military duty he performed 80 years ago, although maybe not exactly the way he recalled it.

Mr. Kuron had to be prompted to talk about his war experiences. But according to his family and friends and the evidence of some old photographs, flight logs and a three-inch shoulder scar he carried to his grave, Mr. Kuron flew a Fokker D-7 fighter biplane on some two dozen combat missions over Russia and France, shooting down three Allied planes and being shot down once himself in France.

As friends recall his account, Mr. Kuron, who was a 19-year-old music and classics student at St. Peter's College in Breslau when he was drafted into the German Air Force in 1914, did not fly in just any of the 81 German fighter squadrons of World War I, but in Wing Commander von Richthofen's own Flight Wing No. 1.

Alas, while there is ample evidence that Mr. Kuron was a German fighter pilot in World War I, and indeed apparently one of the last four survivors, he almost certainly did not fly in the von Richthofen wing.

Peter Kilduff, a New Britain, Conn., historian whose seven books on World War I aviation include the English translation of von Richthofen's memoirs and his definitive biography, checked the meticulously maintained rosters of each of the wing's four squadrons: the blue-tailed 4th, the black-and-white 6th, the yellow-marked 10th, and von Richthofen's own red-flecked 11th led by the all-red Fokker Dr-I triplane that gave the Red Baron his name. The name Kuron, he said, does not appear on any of the lists.

At the same time, after a telephone conversation with Mr. Kuron's daughter, Alwine Kuron of Tewksbury, N.J., who was thumbing through old flight logs, Mr. Kilduff, who has encountered many von Richthofen wing impostors, was convinced that Mr. Kuron had in fact known the Red Baron well.

Whatever the details of his military service, after the war Mr. Kuron returned to the world of music, completing his education, playing piano on German radio and working for an organ company until the rise of Nazism and the first stirrings of anti-Semitism against his Jewish musician friends led him to immigrate to the United States in 1929.

Mr. Kuron, who helped build organs for St. Patrick's Cathedral, Carnegie Hall and churches in Mendham and Madison, N.J., became a United States citizen in 1935 and settled in New Jersey, first in Linden and later in Westfield.

As choirmaster and organist at several Roman Catholic churches until the 1980's, Mr. Kuron became a familiar figure in New Jersey music circles. A man of eclectic musical tastes, he once played "The Merry Widow" on a church organ, startling a priest who could not believe the instrument was capable of such music.

After working in an aviation defense plant in World War II, Mr. Kuron used a stint as a repairman in the Bamberger's department store piano department to start his own lucrative repair business, becoming so indispensable to his private clients that they would not let him retire until he was 92.

A man who arranged chamber concerts for prominent visiting musicians, Mr. Kuron also pursued music as a member, or "knight," of the Schlaraffia, an offbeat German-speaking culture club.

His association with a club that uses medieval mumbo jumbo to spoof 14th-century romanticism suggests that Knight Kuron may have embellished his war record as a tongue-in-cheek elaboration of his association with a fellow knight of the air. Then again, club members may simply have misunderstood his tales of the Red Baron.

At least the Schlaraffians know that his love of music was real. One of his three pianos sits in the club's meeting room in Dover, N.J.

Mr. Kuron's wife, Anne Marie, died in 1989. In addition to his daughter, he is survived by a son from a previous marriage, Gunther of Freehold; seven grandchildren and two great-grandchildren.

November 3, 1997

Charles McCartney,
Known for Travels with Goats,
Dies at 97

You take a fellow who looks like a goat, travels around with goats, eats with goats, lies down among goats and smells like a goat and it won't be long before people will be calling him the Goat Man.

Which is pretty much what Charles McCartney had in mind back in the Depression when he pulled up his Iowa stakes, put on his goatskins, hitched up his ironed-wheeled goat wagon and hit the road for what turned out to be a three-decade odyssey as one of the nation's most endearing eccentrics and by far its most pungent peripatetic roadside tourist attraction.

It is a tribute to the indelible image he created that although he had abandoned the goat life 30 years ago and settled down in a school bus in the south Georgia town of Jeffersonville, outside Macon, when Mr. McCartney died on Nov. 15 in a Macon nursing home, he was still known as the Goat Man. He was 97, or a decade or so younger than he'd taken to claiming to be.

A man given to gross exaggeration when simple embellishment would suffice, Mr. McCartney also claimed to have visited every state except Hawaii: His goats couldn't swim that far, he explained, and if they could, they'd just end up eating the grass skirts off the hula dancers anyway.

Whatever the scope of his travels, Mr. McCartney, who averaged seven miles a day and had a regular route between Iowa and Georgia, spent most of his time creating traffic jams throughout the South, primarily along the old Dixie Highway running through Kentucky, Tennessee, Georgia and Florida.

As many who grew up in the South in the 1940's, 50's and 60's could attest, when the Goat Man came to town it was an event, one that inevitably produced a story and a photograph in the local paper.

Someone would spot him and his 30 or so goats coming down the highway, his wagon piled high with interesting junk, word would get around and pretty soon parents would be driving their children out to meet him, those familiar with the drill taking the precaution of staying upwind of the Goat Man.

As Mr. McCartney, who never took a bath or washed his clothes, once boasted, nobody but his goats could stand the smell of him.

According to research by Darryl Patton and Jimmy Hammett, who collaborated on a 1993 Goat Man video and a 1994 Goat Man book, Mr. McCartney had a colorful life even before he became the Goat Man.

Growing up on a farm outside Sigourney, Iowa, he was considered such an odd child that the family goats were about his only true friends, which helps explain why he took off at 14, married a 24-year-old Spanish knife thrower, served as her exhibition target for a couple of years, then returned to Iowa and married at least twice more.

The last marriage ended when he sold his goat-weary wife for $1,000 to a farmer she'd already grown sweet on.

By then, Mr. McCartney, who had been forced to trade a farm he'd inherited to pay off a grocery bill, had begun his goat excursions, initially taking his wife and young son, Albert Gene, along on short trips and attracting so much attention that he was soon printing up postcards with his picture on them to sell to the gawkers.

(JCH Entertainment)

Toward the end of the 1930's, he struck off on his own, beginning a series of annual circuits and soon making Jeffersonville his home base.

Although the postcards sold so well that rumors actually spread that he was rich, he found a new source of income early in his travels when he stopped off in a backwoods section of north Georgia and had what amounted to an economic epiphany. Observing that the bearded goat man was the spitting image of a figure depicted in religious paintings, some of the deeply religious residents became convinced that he was Jesus Christ and began showering him with gifts.

Mr. McCartney saw no reason to correct them, and by the time the locals, tumbling to the truth, tarred and feathered him and ran him out of town on a rail, the Goat Man had an additional calling: as an itinerant preacher.

Mr. McCartney, who eventually built a church near his school bus in Jeffersonville, admitted that his preaching was a gimmick but insisted it was sincere.

Although his preaching, his wit, his tall tales, his goats and his seeming personification of the totally free life helped make him a beloved figure to many, to others his very strangeness seemed threatening and made him a target of mindless violence, most notably in 1968 in Signal Mountain, Tenn., near Chattanooga, when he was severely beaten by thugs who also slit the throats of eight of his goats.

That was the end of his life as a goat man, but he continued to make occasional hitchhiking forays, including a trip while in his 80's that began when he became obsessed with the actress Morgan Fairchild and ended when he was mugged in Los Angeles.

Although Mr. McCartney, who had lived in the nursing home for 11 years, spoke vaguely about having other children, he leaves no known survivors. His son, Albert Gene, who lived in the school bus in Jeffersonville, was killed there earlier this year.

November 23, 1998

Robert C. Johnston,
Engineer, Is Dead at 85

Robert C. Johnston, who spent almost half a century shaping Manhattan's skyline from below street level and its map from below the water line, died on Dec. 4 at his home in Milbrook, N.Y. He was 85 and had been the foundation engineer in charge of building the 92-acre landfill addition to Manhattan that became Battery Park City.

In a city that sometimes seems defined by the soaring majesty of its lofty spires, it is easy to forget that the towers are not simply plopped down on vacant lots or even constructed from the ground up.

Before you can scrape the sky, you must scoop the earth, and in a city where that is no mean engineering feat, Mr. Johnston was a master in managing the designs of excavations and foundation construction for some of the city's grandest buildings. Among them were United Nations headquarters and the former Chase bank headquarters at 1 Chase Manhattan Plaza.

In a society that lionizes architects, marine and foundation engineering may not seem like a glamorous calling. But Mr. Johnston, whose father was a builder, grew up in the Bronx apparently dreaming of nothing else. By the time he was 14, his wife, Charlotte, recalled last week, he not only knew exactly what he wanted to do but had also picked out the firm he wanted to do it with.

Founded in 1910 by Daniel Moran and long known as Moran & Proctor, the firm, one of the first to work exclusively in marine and foundation engineering, had the field largely to itself.

Mr. Johnston was so determined to become a part of the Moran team that he joined the firm as soon as he graduated from Princeton in 1935. With major construction virtually halted in the Depression, he worked for a year without pay just to be part of the action.

With time out for civil engineering service with the Seabees, including the Normandy landings in World War II, he remained with the firm through a succession of name changes for his entire career, becoming a partner in 1951. When he retired in 1983, the firm, now simply Mueser Rutledge, was known as Mueser, Rutledge, Johnston & DeSimone.

Although he did much of his work in New York, Mr. Johnston had a national reputation. His credits include the Alcoa and United States Steel headquarters buildings in Pittsburgh, and foundations to support heavy aluminum presses used to forge aircraft components in Massachusetts, Ohio, Missouri and California.

In New York, where he worked on the 600-acre industrial park in College Park, Queens, one of his favorite projects was the Chase Manhattan headquarters. To some, the building may seem impressive simply because it soars 60 stories high. To Mr. Johnston's mole's-eye view, what made it special was that it has six levels of basements extending a thrilling 85 feet below street level.

Of all the complex technical problems he solved along the way, by far his most notable achievement did not involve digging a hole, but rather filling up one that did not exist.

By the time he finished, New York had an additional 92 acres, extending for about two miles along the Hudson in lower Manhattan and now the site of two parks, a school and about two dozen apartment and office buildings, including the World Financial Center, all supported by piers driven into the bedrock 70 feet down, beneath the river bed.

The Port Authority gave him a head start by dumping about 1.2 million cubic yards of debris from the World Trade Center excavation into the Hudson, providing about 23.5 acres of what became Battery Park City. But Mr. Johnston, who used sand dredged up from New York Harbor for the rest, had to design around an array of delicate obstacles, including the PATH tubes that cross the site along with the river water intake lines for the Trade Center's cooling system.

In addition to his wife, Mr. Johnston is survived by a daughter, Barbara Adams of Manhattan, and a granddaughter.

Though devoted to his work in a firm that has remained small precisely because its senior partners want to be working engineers rather than administrators, Mr. Johnston rarely worked late and he never took work home to Bronxville, where he lived for many years in a house on Bronxville Road that became a neighborhood attraction because of its colorful profusion of blossoms.

That was because Mr. Johnston, like his wife, was a devoted gardener, one who spent his evenings and weekends planting flowers after his workdays planting skyscrapers.

December 19, 1998

Angelo Zuccotti, 89,

Artist of the Velvet Rope

Angelo Zuccotti, who wielded the velvet rope at El Morocco with such authority and finesse that he helped define the very line between cafe society and social Siberia at New York's most storied supper club, died on Sunday at his home in Cooperstown, N.Y. He was 89 and had operated a bed and breakfast there for the last eight years.

If you were out on the town in the 1950's and 1960's and remember Mr. Zuccotti as a warm and gracious man, almost a cherished friend even though you never exchanged more than a few polite words at a time, it is a safe bet that you were invariably seated at one of the better tables, next to the tiny dance floor, perhaps.

Or maybe even to the right of the entrance at one of the famous zebra-striped banquettes, the signature backdrop of hundreds of magazine and newspaper photographs of visiting Hollywood stars, European royalty and hometown socialites beginning in the 1930's.

On the other hand, if you recall him as an icy and forbidding presence whose piercing blue eyes seemed to look right through you without a glimmer of recognition before he seated you, if he seated you at all, at a table at the left rear, the section known (shudder!) as Siberia, then, as you look back on it, perhaps you were a bit pushy in those days or otherwise failed to live up to Mr. Zuccotti's exacting standards of wealth, beauty and social grace.

Certainly you were not a Bing Crosby, a Cary Grant, a Maurice Chevalier or one of the dozens of other El Morocco regulars Mr. Zuccotti recalled fondly as special favorites.

Whatever their experience, those who saw Mr. Zuccotti as he presided grandly at the El Morocco reservations desk would undoubtedly have been surprised that the tall, slender, distinguished-looking man in white tie and tails who dealt easily and efficiently with the well-dressed throngs emerging from the limousines lining East 54th Street had ridden the subway to work from his home in Greenwich Village and dressed for the evening alongside waiters and bus boys in the basement locker room.

He may have been a working stiff, and Mr. Zuccotti—who was on duty six nights a week and was so devoted to work that his idea of retirement was to operate a rooming house—could hardly deny it, but he also saw his work as an art, one he had been perfecting for years.

A native of Bosco Marengo in the Piedmont section of Italy, Mr. Zuccotti, who came to the United States at age 15 in 1923 and immediately found work in New York's bustling, and often illicit,

(Bill Cunningham)

restaurant industry, was on the El Morocco staff when John Perona, also a Piedmont native, opened it as a speakeasy in 1931.

By the time he succeeded Frank Carino as maître d'hôtel a couple of decades later, Mr. Zuccotti had mastered the formula that had made El Morocco so successful: the creation of social electricity by the adroit and often inspired mixing of disparate people throughout the room.

Mr. Perona likened it to a chef making a sauce. Mr. Zuccotti, who made it a point not to assign tables until customers with reservations actually arrived, had another metaphor.

As he told Frank Borsky for a 1969 article in New York magazine, when he opened El Morocco's walnut doors at 7 P.M. he regarded the room as an empty canvas: "I am the artist and the people are my oils," he said, describing how he would put beautiful women at the front tables next to the dance floor, where they could be seen, while seating celebrities at the banquettes where they would have the pleasure of being recognized.

A master at juggling customers with sometimes outsized and competing egos, Mr. Zuccotti, who was careful to seat divorced couples far apart, could also be relied on for his discretion. Men arriving at El Morocco with girlfriends would be grateful for a whispered warning that their wives were present.

After Mr. Perona died in 1961 and the restaurant was moved from 154 East 54th Street to 307 East 54th Street, Mr. Zuccotti stayed on, providing a measure of social continuity even as cafe society declined and customers would sometimes arrive wearing sports jackets.

After El Morocco closed in 1969, Mr. Zuccotti worked for a while at a resort in the Bahamas, then returned when El Morocco reopened a few years later, the first of a succession of reincarnations.

Mr. Zuccotti, whose first wife died in 1990, is survived by his wife, Laura; two sons, John, a former First Deputy Mayor of New York, and Andrew, a lawyer in Seattle, and five grandchildren.

August 12, 1998

Patsy Southgate,

Who Inspired 50's Literary Paris,

Dies at 70

Patsy Southgate, a writer and translator who helped inspire the literary flowering of Paris in the 1950's and later helped establish the writers' colony on eastern Long Island, becoming a beloved intimate of many of the leading artists of her day, died on July 18 at the Stony Brook University Hospital and Medical Center. A resident of Springs, N.Y., she was 70, and for a decade had been reviewing plays and writing profiles for The East Hampton Star. Her family said the cause was a stroke.

If her own poems, short stories, plays, and an unpublished novel did not put her in a league with the coterie of young writers who gravitated to her orbit in Paris, it was partly because they included such literary luminaries as William Styron, James Baldwin, Richard Wright, Terry Southern, a middle-aged Irwin Shaw and her own husband, Peter Matthiessen.

Even so, Miss Southgate, a woman of fierce intelligence, bitingly funny wit and high-spirited sense of fun, made her mark on literary Paris simply by being her ineffable self.

For one thing, in a city that treasures beauty she was renowned as the most beautiful woman in Paris. A clean-cut American beauty whose finely chiseled features were set off by surprisingly full lips generally framing a dazzling, inviting smile, Miss Southgate, whose animated beauty generally confounded the camera, was blond to her eyelids and had such a steady, open gaze it was said that to look into her deep blue eyes was to fall in love.

In Paris, where falling in love is easy, the only men in the tight-knit American expatriate colony who seemed to have avoided falling in love with her were those who were falling in love with one another, though that was not always sufficient defense against Miss Southgate's captivating charm: On Long Island, she became famous for her deeply loving relationships with gay artists and poets, most notably Frank O'Hara, the poet whose companion, Joe LeSueur, actually moved in with Miss Southgate after Mr. O'Hara's death in 1966.

A native of New York who grew up in Washington, where her father was chief of protocol for the Roosevelt White House, Miss Southgate, a 1950 Smith College graduate, was a perennial pioneer.

A member, along with Mr. Matthiessen, of the first class of the Smith-Yale junior year abroad program that helped establish Paris as a romantic way station for a generation of young Americans, Miss Southgate was ahead of her time even in her vaunted beauty. In an era when the Hollywood ideal was the shapely starlet with an overflowing bosom, her trim form prefigured a later esthetic of sturdy athleticism.

At a time when the young American writers were self-consciously trying to re-create the fabled Paris of F. Scott Fitzgerald, Ernest Hemingway and other 1920's expatriates, Miss Southgate, though sane, was the Zelda Fitzgerald of the 1950's.

But if there was more meaning than madness in her madcap ways, Miss Southgate had her transcendent moments. Once during the tempestuous courtship that preceded their tempestuous marriage, when a row between Miss Southgate and Mr. Matthiessen was followed by a sulking two-day silence followed by an evening phone call that failed to patch things up, Mr. Matthiessen was startled an hour or so later by a late-night banging on the door of his Paris student lodgings.

When his disapproving landlady opened the door to Miss Southgate, who had thrown on her clothes and traveled halfway across Paris after the dispiriting phone call, it took her only a moment to add to her legend as a master of the inspired spontaneous gesture.

"I thought you needed this," she told Mr. Matthiessen as she handed him an orange and departed, leaving him to marvel, as he still does, that it was exactly what he needed.

After marrying, graduating and returning to Paris in 1951, the Matthiessens were instant leaders of a bohemian life that included legendary late-night revels at the Café de Tournon, Le Champlain or the Dome. Even their apartment, a multilevel, Paris-perfect studio walk-up at 14 Rue Perceval with a balcony overlooking the Montparnasse rail yards, became the stuff of legend.

Mr. Styron made it a major setting for his 1960 novel, "Set This House on Fire," and it was there that Mr. Matthiessen and Harold L. Humes founded The Paris Review, summoning Mr. Matthiessen's boyhood friend, George Plimpton, from his studies at Cambridge University to run it.

For all the publication's later acclaim, it is an open question whether the writers who gathered there would have been as willing to discuss the harebrained scheme if Miss Southgate had not been present as additional lure.

After Miss Southgate gave birth in 1952 to a child who lived only 12 hours, the couple took the precaution of moving to a ground-floor apartment for her next pregnancy, so she would not have to walk up stairs. Their son, Lucas, and The Paris Review both came out in the spring of 1953, with both parents represented by French translations.

Before the year was out they had returned to the United States and settled on Long Island, where as practically the only writers in the vicinity they fell in almost by default with their neighbor Jackson Pollock and other artists.

After the couple were divorced in 1956, Miss Southgate, whose later marriage to the artist Mike Goldberg also ended in divorce, became a fixture in the Long Island art scene, forming close friendships with Willem de Kooning, Larry Rivers and other acclaimed painters even as she continued her own work, contributing to The Evergreen Review, translating a series of books from French and eventually finding her late-life niche with The East Hampton Star.

While her fabled beauty faded, her appeal did not. At her death, her hair was as blond as ever and her eyes just as blue.

She is survived by two children, Lucas and Sara Matthiessen, both of East Northport, and two grandsons.

July 26, 1998

HENRY GOURDINE DIES AT 94;

MASTER OF FISHING SKILLS AND LORE

Henry L. Gourdine, who spent his life messing about in boats, becoming a Hudson River legend for his passionate, lifelong love of the river, his skills as a commercial fisherman and the delight he took in passing on his lore, died on Oct. 17 at Phelps Memorial Hospital Center in Sleepy Hollow, N.Y. He was 94 and lived in Ossining, N.Y.

To the few dozen fishermen who still make a living netting shad from the Hudson, Mr. Gourdine was the dean of the commercial fishermen, a man who took up his profession in 1920 at the age of 17 and never really abandoned it. On the day he died, he was working on nets in his basement.

To schoolchildren who flocked to his demonstrations of ancient skills, he was the net doctor, the old man with the magnetic personality and a satchel filled with needles and other tools he would use to teach them how to mend nets while enthralling them with stories from the old days.

For much of his life, Mr. Gourdine was simply one of hundreds of commercial fishermen who netted shad during the spring spawning season and harvested river-fattened striped bass in the fall.

Not that many of them did it as well as Mr. Gourdine, a river-going perfectionist who built his own boats, cut and trimmed trees into the poles that anchored his nets and became famous for his knowledge of the river and his innovative experiments in fishing techniques.

In recent years, with striped bass banned to commercial fishermen because of toxic contamination with PCB's and with the river's shad supply sharply reduced by ocean shad fishing, he had become something of a living museum, a man cherished by fishermen and conservationists for his devotion to the river.

As Gov. George E. Pataki put it, he was "a state treasure."

Mr. Gourdine, who was born at Croton Point, N.Y., attributed his love of the Hudson to growing up in a house built so close to the river that waves lapped at the foundation.

When he was a toddler, he liked to recall, his mother would tie a rope around his waist to keep him from falling into the water, or in his case, perhaps, to keep him from jumping in. He became such a river rat, to the neglect of his household chores, that when he was 10, his mother made him wear a red dress, hoping it would shame him into staying away from his friends at the river. It worked, but only for a few days.

Mr. Gourdine got his first boating experiences as a child rowing to the Underhill brickworks with his father, who operated the factory steam engine and whose duties included firing up the boiler at 5:30 A.M. On the days he let his son pull the steam whistle to awaken the other workers, everyone in earshot would know that little Henry was on the job. As Mr. Gourdine recalled it, it was easy to lift a child up to the handle, but not so easy to get him to let go.

As a commercial fisherman who had as many as a dozen men working for him in three crews, he was the consummate professional. As deft with an ax as he was with nets, Mr. Gourdine, who worked as a carpenter between fishing seasons, would sharpen his poles to such a finely tapered point that they would look as if they had gone through a giant pencil sharpener.

And when it came to winching a line of them into the river bottom to hold his nets, Mr. Gourdine had a carpenter's eye. Other fishermen might set their poles in a squiggly line. His would be string-straight.

As an independent commercial fisherman, Mr. Gourdine experienced the ebb and flow of the industry as prices fluctuated and the supplies of fish receded and surged, sometimes from season to season.

After one flush year, Mr. Gourdine recalled, he began the next season riding to the river in a Cadillac. When the season was over, he said, he walked home.

He had his glory days, to be sure: Once, in the 1930's, he and his crew unloaded 12,000 pounds of fish on Crawbuckie Beach from a single netting, a huge haul but a mixed blessing. It took so long to pack the catch for shipment to the Fulton Fish Market, the men were too exhausted to set their nets on the next tide.

Always in demand as a skilled carpenter, Mr. Gourdine was fastidious about telling prospective employers that come April, he would be gone fishing. Some doubted that a man would walk away from a secure job for the uncertainties of the river, but as soon as the shad started running, Mr. Gourdine would be gone so fast, as he put it, that he would leave his hammer "hanging in the air."

Mr. Gourdine's wife died in 1979. He is survived by two daughters, Jean G. Drumgold and Lydia Yvonne Spencer; a son, Harry Norman, and a sister, Esther Nabors, all of Ossining; six grandchildren and a great-grandson.

October 26, 1997

George W. Crockett Dies at 88;
Was a Civil Rights Crusader

George W. Crockett Jr., a civil rights warrior who went over the top so often in the battle for racial justice that he earned a decade of bemused retirement in Congress, died on Sept. 7 at a hospice near his home in Washington. He was 88 and had represented a Detroit district in the House of Representatives from 1980 to 1991.

In the quest for racial equality, Mr. Crockett often operated so far beyond the trenches that it was often decades before society caught up.

As the first hearing officer of the wartime Fair Employment Practices Committee, for example, he regularly ordered companies to adopt race-neutral hiring and promotion policies that would not become standard until the 1970's.

As a lawyer in 1949 representing 11 Communist leaders accused of violating the Smith Act, he presented such a vigorous defense of the right of free speech and association that he served four months in jail for contempt of court. Years later, the Supreme Court gutted the Smith Act's strongest provisions, and the 1949 prosecution itself came to be viewed by many as an embarrassing relic of an aberrant era.

And as a judge in Detroit in the 1960's and 1970's, he freed so many black defendants and handed out so many lenient sentences, refusing to countenance police brutality, that he became a hero to the local black population even as he was widely castigated by the white press.

A native of Jacksonville, Fla., who graduated from Morehouse College and received a law degree from the University of Michigan before entering private practice, first in Jacksonville and later in West Virginia, Mr. Crockett went to Washington in 1940 as a protégé of West Virginia's Senator Matthew M. Neely, the man who had converted him from a Lincoln Republican to a New Deal Democrat.

Although he had been assured a position with the Justice Department, Mr. Crockett was shunted to the Labor Department, holding a series of posts that convinced him that black Americans and American workers were often fellow victims of an oppressive society.

A chance meeting with a top official of the United Auto Workers led to a job organizing and running a union fair-employment division.

It was through his work with the union in Detroit that Mr. Crockett was asked to join the team defending the 11 Communist leaders, including the head of the Michigan Communist Party. Before accepting the offer, Mr. Crockett read both the Smith Act and the Constitution and decided the two were incompatible.

Although he had no interest in Communism, Mr. Crockett savored and even courted the notoriety the case brought him, once describing the Communist Party as the conscience of America and forever pointing out that it was the only party that demanded full equality for black Americans.

After narrowly avoiding disbarment because of his contempt conviction, Mr. Crockett, who had become something of a hero to civil libertarians, helped to organize Michigan's first integrated law firm and later ran the legal defense arm of the Mississippi voting project—an experience that left him shaken after three young people he asked to investigate a church burning were lynched and buried in a dam.

After an abortive race for the Detroit City Council, he was elected in 1966 to Detroit's criminal court, known there as the Recorder's Court, and became an outspoken practitioner of equal justice in a system that regularly trampled on the rights of poor black defendants.

Although he could be tough on defendants convicted of serious crimes that harmed innocent victims, he regularly freed first offenders, gave lenient sentences to those convicted of minor offenses and was once so outraged that a real criminal had been beaten by the police that he let the man go free, announcing that he had suffered enough.

Convinced that black judges had to lead the fight for equal justice, he also helped organize the National Bar Association's Judicial Council, with some 400 black judges now.

In 1969, when he was awakened with the news that a Detroit policeman had been killed by a sniper firing from a church during a meeting of black separatists and that the police had shot their way into the church and seized some 140 people, holding them in the police garage pending chemical tests to determine if any had recently fired a gun, Judge Crockett did not wait for the case to come to him.

He went to the police station, declared court in session and began freeing prisoners he determined were being held without probable cause, allowing only a handful to be retained in custody, making him a hero to the local black population.

Just how much of a hero became apparent in 1980 when, at the age of 71 after retiring from the bench, he won a sinecure in the House of Representatives with 98 percent of the vote. He held the seat for five terms with only slightly reduced majorities, even though he made it a point not to introduce a single bill.

He did introduce a couple of resolutions denouncing South African apartheid and was duly arrested while picketing the South African Embassy, but his only bid for the spotlight came when he sought appointment as chairman of the Foreign Affairs subcommittee on the Western Hemisphere.

The quest predictably drew a wave of hysterical denunciations from right-wing groups questioning his loyalty, but with the backing of the black caucus, Mr. Crockett prevailed and had the satisfaction later of being named by President Ronald Reagan as a citizen delegate to a United Nations session.

And before he retired in 1991, the man who liked to be out in front of controversial issues had become the first member of Congress to call for the decriminalization of drugs.

Mr. Crockett is survived by his second wife, Dr. Harriet Clark Harris; three children from his first marriage, George 3d, a judge on the Recorder's Court in Detroit, Elizabeth Ann Hicks of Los Angeles, and Dr. Ethelene Jones of Detroit; two stepsons, Dr. Cleveland Robert Chambliss Jr. of Atlanta and Marque Chambliss of Mountain View, Calif.; a sister, Alzeda Hacker of Pittsburgh; eight grandchildren and four great-grandchildren.

September 15, 1997

David Longaberger,

Basket Maker, Dies at 64

Dave Longaberger, a born basket weaver and business visionary who figured out that the way to make basket weaving pay was to get a lot of other people to do the weaving and a lot more to do the selling, died on Wednesday at his home outside Newark, Ohio. He was 64 and had turned a small basket-weaving venture into a $700 million-a-year business even as he transformed a slice of central Ohio into a sprawling theme park based on Longaberger baskets.

His family said the cause was kidney cancer.

There is no denying the charm of an old-fashioned hardwood maple basket, especially one made by hand and signed and dated by the maker. Still, it seems far-fetched to suppose that there would be a modern-day demand for more than eight million such baskets a year, or that they would become such sought-after collectors' items that they would support a flourishing Internet trade with more than 1,000 Web sites.

Then again, Mr. Longaberger was a master of the far-fetched. He was, after all, the man who celebrated the success of his Longaberger Company, which was based in Newark, by building as his corporate headquarters a $30 million, seven-story structure in the form of a market basket, complete with a pair of 75-ton handles on the roof.

Even his childhood was far-fetched. The son and grandson of basket weavers, Mr. Longaberger was born in the little town of Dresden, about 25 miles northeast of Newark, and grew up in a house with three bedrooms, one bathroom and 12 children, all schooled in basket weaving by their father, J. W. Longaberger, who made baskets for local potters and farmers.

Mr. Longaberger, who got a job stocking grocery store shelves when he was 6, always demonstrated a certain tenacity. Partly because he had a severe stutter and suffered from epilepsy, he repeated the first grade, was held back in the fifth grade twice and did not graduate from high school until he was 21.

After holding a series of jobs, including one as a Fuller Brush salesman, and serving in the Army, he began his business career by buying and operating a small restaurant in Dresden and later acquiring a local grocery store and pharmacy.

It was not until 1973 that Mr. Longaberger, noticing that baskets were becoming popular in shopping malls, began his basket business, coaxing his father out of retirement and taking on four other weavers.

Sales were so sluggish in the first years that in 1978, he revamped his business. Taking the Tupperware page from the direct-sales book, he enlisted sales associates to hold Longaberger basket parties and added an Amway twist, giving associates a percentage of the commissions earned by associates they recruited.

The appeal of the baskets and the standard sales pitch, which

(The Longaberger Company)

170

incorporated lore of the Longaberger family and the Dresden basket-weaving tradition, were so powerful that the business grew rapidly. Today the company employs 7,000 people, including 1,500 weavers, and there are more than 47,000 salespeople.

In addition to 80 styles and sizes of baskets, which sell for $25 to $150, the company also sells, but does not make, pottery, wrought-iron products, curtain fabrics and bedding. But it is the baskets that have made Longaberger a household name.

From the beginning, the women who bought the baskets were so enamored of them that they began making pilgrimages to Dresden, which Mr. Longaberger obligingly turned into a tourist town, complete with Longaberger restaurants, Longaberger shops and a Longaberger museum.

A man who gave away millions of dollars, Mr. Longaberger bought and restored several Dresden buildings and even provided new sidewalks.

When the company outgrew Dresden, Mr. Longaberger moved its main operations a few miles down State Road 16 to Frazeysburg, which also became a tourist destination, as Newark did, in turn, when the Longaberger basket building opened at the end of 1997. An estimated 500,000 tourists visit the area each year.

After his cancer was diagnosed two years ago, Mr. Longaberger promoted his elder daughter, Tami of Zanesville, to company president and put his other daughter, Rachel of New Albany, in charge of the family foundation.

Although Tami Longaberger seems to be a shrewd manager, it remains to be seen whether she, or anyone else, can match her father's soaring vision. She tried to talk her father out of building the basket building.

In addition to his daughters, Mr. Longaberger, who was married and divorced twice, is survived by his mother, Bonnie of Dresden; six sisters, Genevieve Hard of Thornville, Ohio, Wendy Little of Dresden, Mary Ann McCafferty of Frazeysburg, Judy Swope of Dresden, Ginny Lou Wilcox of Dresden and Carmen Fortney of Dresden; five brothers, Larry of Newark and Jerry, Rich, Gary and Jeff, all of Dresden, and five grandchildren.

March 22, 1999

Manuel Elizalde, 60, Dies;

Defender of Primitive Tribe

Manuel Elizalde Jr., a wealthy Filipino official who caused a sensation in 1971 when he announced that he had discovered a tiny tribe of people who had lived for thousands of years in such blissful Stone Age isolation that they had no word for war, died on Saturday at his home in Makati, a Manila suburb. He was 60, and some scientists say he was one of the world's master hoaxers.

His family gave no cause of death.

To the wave of anthropologists, archaeologists and others who descended on Mindanao, in the southern Philippines, in the early 1970's, the 24 people Mr. Elizalde said he had found there in June 1971 seemed too good to be true.

Calling themselves Tasadays, after their sacred mountain, they were hunter-gatherers who never ventured far from their cave dwellings, had no notion of agriculture, went around naked or in leaves, lived in perfect harmony and said they had assumed they were the only people in the world, even though a population of farming people lived only a three-hour walk through the dense jungle.

There were those who were suspicious from the beginning. For one thing, Mr. Elizalde was something of an iconoclast. A Harvard-educated scion of one of the Philippines' wealthiest families, he had given up his hard-drinking playboy ways to champion the nation's beleaguered minorities, first as a private citizen and later as a member of President Ferdinand E. Marcos's Cabinet.

Mr. Elizalde affected such an interest in primitive youth that he and his wife adopted 50 children from minority groups.

He was also something of a publicity hound. By the time he

learned of the Tasadays, from a hunter who had stumbled on them some years earlier, he had already made a name for himself—and some powerful enemies—by defending the nation's primitive minorities from the incursions of loggers and other commercial interests.

Still, the initial wave of social scientists who visited the Tasadays were convinced they were who they and Mr. Elizalde said they were. Their enthusiastic reports led to a book, "The Gentle Tasaday: A Stone Age People in the Philippine Rain Forest," by John Nance; glowing accounts in The National Geographic, and extensive television coverage.

Expressing fear that the Tasadays' habitat would be destroyed by the encroachments of civilization, the Marcos Government created a 46,000-acre preserve for them and put it off limits to loggers and farmers.

Skeptics were dismayed in 1974 when Mr. Elizalde, citing a need to protect the Tasadays from exploitation and the harmful effects of too much contact with civilization, blocked any further visits by social scientists.

The area remained off limits until after Marcos was deposed in 1986. Then, as outsiders again made their way to the Tasaday preserve, doubts about them became rampant.

Some anthropologists had called their story implausible from the beginning. Among other things, they pointed out, their caves lacked the middens, or trash heaps, that would have been expected of peoples living there for centuries.

It did not help when members of a neighboring tribe said Mr. Elizalde had paid them to take off their clothes and pose as Tasadays for visiting journalists and others.

Mr. Elizalde, who had been forced to leave the Philippines in 1983 after a falling-out with Imelda Marcos, the President's wife, settled on a coffee plantation in Costa Rica with more than a dozen young Filipino girls. It did not add to his reputation when the Costa Rica Government expelled him in 1986, citing scandalous reports of what went on inside his heavily guarded compound.

He returned to the Philippines in 1988, helped manage his family's extensive business interests and tried unsuccessfully to rekindle his political career. A 1993 nomination to be Ambassador to Mexico was withdrawn after it created a political furor over Mr. Elizalde's ties to the Marcos administration and his role in what was then widely perceived as the Tasaday hoax.

Since 1971 the Tasadays have virtually merged into neighboring groups and picked up so many trappings of modern civilization that they can no longer be studied as unique primitives.

But the debate over their origins still rages. For all the questions of plausibility and the reports that they were paid to fake the degree of their primitive status, some social scientists still believe they had lived for a few centuries in complete isolation.

It was a reflection of their rapid acculturalization that in 1988, several members of the tribe filed a libel suit against anthropologists who had called them fakers.

"We are the forest," one of the women said before affixing her thumbprint to the complaint. "We are the Tasaday. We are as real as the forest and the flowers and the trees and the stream."

It was an eloquent declaration, and one that would undoubtedly have been given more credence if it had not been made at Mr. Elizalde's Manila mansion by an interpreter he supplied.

His survivors include two sons, Manuel 3d and Miguel; a daughter, Mia, and a brother.

May 8, 1997

David Ludlum,

Weather Expert, Dies at 86

David M. Ludlum, a scholar who never lost his boyhood delight
in the magic of snow, died on Friday at his home in Princeton, N.J.
He was 86 and the nation's foremost historian of American
weather.

The cause was complications after a stroke, his family said.

Mr. Ludlum's bright yellow Victorian house in Princeton had
become a local landmark: the home of a kindly, apple-cheeked
man whose savvy scanning of the skies and expert readings of the
instruments in his fully equipped backyard beehive weather station made him the resident expert on whether it would rain on a
neighborhood picnic, a town parade or a university commence-
ment.

But long before he began turning out a series of books detailing the history of Colonial America hurricane by hard winter, and
long before he was calling the turn of battle in World War II as the
commander of an Army Air Forces meteorological unit, David
Ludlum was a little boy in East Orange, N.J., catching snowflakes
on his tongue and making angels in the snow.

A New York stockbroker's son, Mr. Ludlum was so enchanted
by every aspect of snow, from its magical transformation of his
neighborhood to its prospects for sleighing, skating and skiing, that
predicting snowfalls to come and measuring those at hand became
his consuming hobby.

From the beginning, there was a scholarly component to his
interest, and with no well-established meteorological career path
to follow, Mr. Ludlum pursued scholarship instead, majoring in
American history at Princeton, receiving a master's degree from

the University of California at Berkeley and then returning to Princeton for a doctorate just in time to face a Depression job drought.

Grateful for a chance to teach high school history, he joined the faculty of the Peddie School in Hightstown, N.J., but his life as Mr. Chips lasted only three years.

After the Nazi storm broke in Europe, and Mr. Ludlum sensed the war clouds gathering in the United States, he enlisted in the Army in January 1941 (a step ahead of the draft) and used his prerogative as a volunteer to secure a place in a meteorological unit. As he later recalled, every other man inducted with him was sent to the Philippines, many to die on Bataan a year later, just as Mr. Ludlum was completing intensive training as a battlefield weather forecaster.

Commanding a front-line forecasting unit that fought across North Africa, through Sicily and up the boot of Italy, Mr. Ludlum, who rose to the rank of lieutenant colonel, became a footnote to military history in 1944. At that time, military planners asked him to predict the weather for the intricate air and land assault on the German fortress at Monte Cassino, Italy.

Mr. Ludlum had shaken his head so many times at 5 P.M. briefing after 5 P.M. briefing that the oft-postponed assault was given the official code name of Operation Ludlum. On the 21st day, Feb. 14, Mr. Ludlum said yes. The next day, the monastery at Monte Cassino and much of the surrounding area was bombed to destruction, and three months later Allied troops entered Rome.

A decade later, Mr. Ludlum portrayed himself in an obscure Paramount Pictures documentary, "From Cassino to Korea." By this time, he had established himself as a leading civilian weather expert and entrepreneur.

It is testament to his foresight that a man who once defined weather as something that everybody talks about and nobody invests in made a more than comfortable living as the founder of Systems Associates in Princeton, the nation's first weather instrument sales company.

Mr. Ludlum also found it well worth three decades of weekends to single-handedly publish Weatherwise, a magazine for weather enthusiasts that he founded in 1948 and that is now published by the Heldref Foundation in Washington.

While researching his doctoral dissertation, later published as "Social Ferment in Vermont: 1791–1850," Mr. Ludlum had become fascinated with accounts of weather conditions in old Vermont newspapers. After the war he resumed this research with scholarly zeal, poring over old letters and crumbling diaries and turning out a series of books with names like "Early American Winters," "Early American Hurricanes," "The American Weather Book," "The Weather Record Book," "The Weather Factor" and "The New Jersey Weather Book."

Although he owned what is believed to be the only full set of National Weather Service records in private hands, Mr. Ludlum, noting that the Weather Service was founded in 1870, drew the scholarly line there. Anything after 1870 was the Government's responsibility, he figured. Everything earlier was his, including the hurricane warning Christopher Columbus issued in 1502 and the Northeast's harshest and longest 18th-century winter, 1780, when ships were locked in more than a foot of ice in the harbor in New London, Conn., on May 10.

In recent years, Mr. Ludlum, who sold his business in 1978, had slowed down a bit, but his enthusiasm remained keen. As his daughter, Carol Collier, noted, he could watch the Weather Channel for hours at a time, especially in the winter, when—who knows—the very next cold front could bring snow.

In addition to his daughter, of Trappe, Pa., he is survived by his wife, Rita; four sons, Kenneth, of Hillsborough, Calif., David A., of Manhattan, Peter, of Mission Viejo, Calif., and Stephen, of Newton, Mass., and eight grandchildren.

May 29, 1997

HOWARD HIGMAN,
ACADEMIC IMPRESARIO, DIES AT 80

Howard Higman, the agile-minded academic impresario whose annual World Affairs conferences at the University of Colorado attracted a dazzling and diverse array of fun-loving intellectuals, died on Nov. 22 at Boulder Community Hospital. He was 80.

Officially, Mr. Higman was a sociology professor, but that was merely an academic cover for his role as the thinking person's Nathan Detroit, the founder and proprietor of the oldest established permanent freewheeling gabfest in academia, a weeklong extravaganza of discussion and debate that was once compared to a cross between a think tank and a fraternity party.

Whatever it was, it lasted 47 years.

Lured by the chance to meet and debate articulate, quick-witted specialists from different backgrounds and disciplines, the conference's participants over the years included such diverse personalities as Eleanor Roosevelt, Henry A. Kissinger, Abba Eban, Henry Steele Commager, Buckminster Fuller, Marshall McLuhan, Brian Wilson of the Beach Boys, Arthur Miller, Ted Turner, Ralph Nader and Roger Ebert, a perennially popular panelist who proved he could hold his own with the reigning resident wits when he inverted Veblen to sum up the weeklong conference as "the leisure of the theory class."

Mr. Higman, the son of a miner turned contractor, was born in a hospital on the University of Colorado campus and grew up, as he once acknowledged, wanting to know everything. A brilliant man known both for the breadth and depth of his knowledge, he apparently majored in art as a Colorado undergraduate and then switched to sociology in its graduate school only because everything-there-is-to-know was not a recognized discipline. Although Mr. Higman served on various government committees over the years and spent four years directing a Vista training program, his abiding passion was the conference, which he started as a young instructor in part to offer students at Colorado, known at the time as a party school, an alternative to skiing—thinking.

The conference, which began with a single speaker in 1948, was originally designed as a one-shot tribute to the United Nations, but it proved so popular that the university ordered Mr. Higman to make it an annual event.

It attracted major attention in 1953, the height of Senator Joseph McCarthy's anti-communist crusade, when Mr. Higman stacked the panels with speakers who turned the conference into a continuous attack on the Senator's tactics.

A measure of the conference's popularity was that the 125 invited participants not only received no stipends for spending a week serving on one panel discussion after another, but also had to pay their way to Boulder. There, at least, room, board and local transportation were provided. The panelists bunked with local families and were driven around town by Colorado students who also served as waiters, bartenders and awed acolytes.

Like an astute hostess who makes it a point to seat the duchess next to the dustman, Mr. Higman, who once arranged a debate between Timothy Leary and G. Gordon Liddy, was a master at orchestrating creative tensions. Among other things, he required participants to take part in at least one discussion on a topic they knew nothing about. And to insure that his panelists would talk about what they knew and not what they had boned up on, he made it a point not to disclose the list of topics or panel assignments until after the participants had gathered in Boulder.

The subjects of the 200 overlapping panel discussions could be profound ("Third World Development—Women as a Force of Change") or prophylactic ("The Resurgent Condom").

Such a rich smorgasbord attracted 30,000 townspeople and Colorado students each year. Even so, the university suspended the conference this year, saying it had gotten out of touch with its student interests.

A chief attraction of the conference was Mr. Higman himself, a man of such enormous intellectual range that he taught himself architecture and gardening because he could not afford to hire skilled professionals, and, for the same reason, made himself into an accomplished French chef.

For all his brilliance, Mr. Higman could also be something of an absentminded professor. During a stay with a friend in Washington, for example, he once cooked an elaborate meal for 30 guests, but forgot to invite anybody, leaving his host, John Midgley, to eat beef Wellington for three weeks.

Known as everything from dictatorial to lovable, Mr. Higman could sometimes be impatient with the world, especially when it failed to keep up with his own inventive mind. Unwilling to wait for the development of portable telephones, for example, he had 17 telephones installed in his house so one would always be handy.

He is survived by his wife, Marion, and three daughters, Anne and Elizabeth of Boulder, and Alice Reich of Denver.

December 1, 1995

Sadler Hayes, 86, Salesman of Insurance and a Partygoer

Sadler Hayes, a music-minded insurance agent who was a mainstay of the North Carolina Society in New York City for more than 60 years, died on Saturday at Lenox Hill Hospital. He was 86.

His family said the cause was a heart attack.

From the time he arrived in New York from North Carolina in the early 1930's and fell in with the hard-partying, polo-playing regulars who hung out at the Squadron A Armory on East 94th Street, Mr. Hayes was the life of just about every party he ever went to.

A self-taught musician who mastered the recorder, the guitar, the trumpet, and, more or less, the flute, Mr. Hayes, who also sang, never had to be asked twice to perform.

If he was feeling diffident, he would arrive with his recorder stuck in the back pocket of his tuxedo. In a more expansive mood he would have his guitar slung over his shoulder. Either way, if anybody needed serenading, before the evening was over Mr. Hayes was sure to oblige, unless he was otherwise engaged, sitting in with the band.

Although he rode well and loved horses so much that he once kept a favorite mount overnight in his East Side apartment, there was reason to believe that it was his love of music more than his devotion to the National Guard cavalry regiment that attracted Mr. Hayes to Squadron A.

He became his troop's bugler and held the post with the

squadron and its alumni social arm, the Squadron A Association, for more than 50 years.

At the association's black-tie banquet in 1986, Mr. Hayes, who summoned the troop to dinner with a gleaming brass Wurlitzer bugle that had been used in Cuba in the Spanish-American War, expounded on the value of the bugle for battlefield communication, recalling that "Custer didn't have a bugler."

Mr. Hayes was a native of Charlotte, N.C., who was forced to drop out of the University of North Carolina in the Depression. He found an insurance job in New York. He had intended to return to North Carolina, but found he didn't have to. There were so many Tar Heels in New York, he discovered, it was possible to have a full down-home social life without leaving Manhattan.

Joining the North Carolina Society, founded in 1897, Mr. Hayes became so active he was known as Mr. North Carolina in New York.

In addition to offering an opportunity for compatible company (and to generate life insurance business), the association's annual banquets had a special appeal. The several hundred members included alumni of the state's various colleges, each with its own songs, so Mr. Hayes, who had learned the words to all of them, would be singing all night.

Mr. Hayes established himself as one of the country's top life insurance salesmen. His work made him wealthy, because he was a highly gregarious salesman of considerable charm, and because he had a legion of loyal and well-heeled friends.

In philanthropy, the Hayes version had musical overtones. Concerned with illiteracy, he had a brainstorm. Recognizing that decoding one set of symbols was very much like decoding another, he hit on teaching youngsters to read music to prepare them to read words.

To put his ideas into practice, Mr. Hayes, a onetime director of the Third Street Music School Settlement, helped found the Diller-Quaile-Brick Church summer music program for children.

Teaching children to read music had another appeal to Mr. Hayes. It kept the music going.

Mr. Hayes is survived by his wife, Agnes; a daughter, Alice, of

Charlotte, and a son, John, of New Hempstead, N.Y.; a sister, Eleanor Barnhardt of Charlotte; two brothers, Robert, of Concord, N.C., and Francis, of Charlotte, and three grandsons.

January 22, 1997

Mary Bancroft

Dead at 93;

U.S. Spy in World War II

Mary Bancroft, a Boston Brahmin colleen who cut a coquettish swath through 20th-century history, bewitching men of power even as she did brilliant work as an American spy in Switzerland in World War II, died on Jan. 10 at her Fifth Avenue apartment. She was 93.

If Mary Bancroft had not existed, a hack novelist would surely have invented her, or tried.

Dime-store fiction could undoubtedly have accommodated her cliché origins as the daughter of a patrician, Harvard-trained lawyer and a distinctly déclassé Irish girl, who died in childbirth, setting up her father's marriage to a disapproving, if not quite wicked, stepmother.

He left his daughter to be reared by a paternal grandmother with such a haughty and virulent disdain for the Irish that it was years before Miss Bancroft learned that the woman had herself been an Irish working girl before marrying into the august Bancroft family.

It would have taken a Dickens to invent Nolan, the Bancroft coachman who became Miss Bancroft's constant childhood companion, sharing her delight in the day's news, especially of war and disaster.

And a Dickens could even have contrived for her father's second wife to be the stepdaughter of Clarence Barron, the short, rotund powerhouse owner of The Wall Street Journal who encouraged his step-granddaughter to meet and study people of all walks of life, "even gamblers and crooks," and who gave her what became her credo as a sometime journalist and spy: "Facts are not the truth but only indicate where the truth may lie."

A novelist might have foreseen that a daring, restless woman would find Smith College such a bore that she would escape after a year into what turned out to be a stultifying marriage to a teenage chum and then divorce and seek refuge in another loveless marriage, this time to a Swiss businessman.

But it would have taken a remarkable visionary to have imagined Miss Bancroft's later life as an accomplished spy, a woman with such penetrating intelligence, infallible intuition and boundless verve—not to mention legs that rarely failed to draw a second glance—that her intellectual, emotional or romantic conquests included Carl Jung, Woody Allen and Henry R. Luce.

To Jung, the psychologist who became her confidant during her years in Switzerland, her appeal was textbook obvious. In his scheme of things she was an extroverted intuitive, one who had experienced such fierce inter-family battles for her affections as a child that power had become her natural element. She had such an instinctive knack for wielding it, he told her, that men seeking or holding power would cherish her advice, as indeed they did.

Her relationships were often platonic, apparently—and surprisingly—including even her postwar fling in New York with Luce, the Time Inc. founder and a legendary ladies' man.

But as her own 1983 book, "Autobiography of a Spy," makes explicit, her wartime romance with Allen Dulles, the American spymaster who laid the groundwork for the Central Intelligence Agency with his brilliant successes in Switzerland in World War II, was as torrid as they come.

At the time, Miss Bancroft's second marriage was beginning to unravel, and Mr. Dulles, whose wife was in the United States, was looking for recruits to interview the hundreds of refugees, adventurers and spies who poured into officially neutral Switzerland from every corner of wartime Europe.

Impressed with the insightful analyses of German articles and speeches she had prepared for one of his associates, he sought her out, quickly concluding that she would be an ideal operative, and more.

"It should work out very well," he blurted out on their second meeting. "We can let the work cover the romance—and the romance cover the work." The remark might have seemed startling considering that the subject of romance had not been mentioned, but Mr. Dulles was as perceptive as his recruit. The logic appealed to her, and so did he.

In what became a regular routine, she would help him prepare his legendary nightly telephone reports to Washington at his home in Bern, and then the two would engage in what she called "a bit of dalliance."

As a spy, she interviewed and sized up visitors from Germany and German-occupied territory, sometimes with startling results. One contact provided the first inkling that a previously unknown figure named Joseph Broz had become the man to deal with in Yugoslavia, where he was known as Tito.

When her German maid's brother-in-law wrote from the Russian front asking for an aluminum spoon, noting that his wife had told him none was available in Germany, she picked up a critical clue about the war's effects on German production.

By far her most important work was with Hans Bernd Gisevius, a top officer of German military intelligence, who was not only a key figure in a vast plot to kill Hitler and set up a civilian democracy but who, well in advance of what turned out to be a bungled assassination attempt on July 20, 1944, had supplied a manuscript detailing the conspiracy.

Miss Bancroft was entrusted with translating the manuscript into English (Gisevius wanted it published immediately after the coup), but her real job was to make sure he was not a double agent (she concluded he was not) and then to elicit and pass on the detailed information he supplied about the day-to-day shifts of power and strategy within the German Government.

After the war, her daughter said, Miss Bancroft settled in New York, wrote a few novels, lectured on Jung, became active in local Democratic politics, became friends with Woody Allen and became Luce's confidante.

When her daughter, Mary Jane, married Horace Taft, the son of Senator Robert A. Taft of Ohio, the wedding pictures were published in Life—"a present from Luce," Mrs. Taft said.

In addition to her daughter, of Atlanta, Miss Bancroft is survived by 6 grandchildren and 12 great-grandchildren.

January 19, 1997

ROBERT McG. THOMAS JR., 60,

CHRONICLER OF UNSUNG LIVES

By Michael T. Kaufman

Robert McG. Thomas Jr., a reporter for The New York Times who extended the possibilities of the conventional obituary form, shaking the dust from one of the most neglected areas of daily journalism, died on Thursday at his family's summer home in Rehoboth Beach, Del. He was 60 and also had a home in Manhattan.

The cause was abdominal cancer, said his wife, Joan.

Mr. Thomas began writing obituaries full time in 1995 after serving as a police reporter, a rewrite man, a society news reporter and a sports writer. He developed a fresh approach to the genre, looking for telling details to illuminate lives that might otherwise have been overlooked or underreported.

Mr. Thomas saw himself as the sympathetic stranger at the wake listening to the friends and survivors of the deceased, alert for the moment when one of them would tell a memorable tale that could never have made its way into Who's Who or a résumé but that just happened to define a life.

In 1995, when The Times proposed him for a Pulitzer Prize in the category of spot news, the nomination began: "Every week, readers write to The New York Times to say they were moved to tears or laughter by an obituary of someone they hadn't known until that morning's paper. Invariably, the obituary is the work of Robert McG. Thomas Jr., who hadn't known the subject, either, until the assignment landed on his desk a few hours before deadline."

The gallery of portraits that Mr. Thomas compiled covered an impressive range. Among them were Howard C. Fox, "the Chicago clothier and sometime big-band trumpeter who claimed credit for creating and naming the zoot suit with the reet pleat, the reave sleeve, the ripe stripe, the stuff cuff and the drape shape that was the stage rage during the boogie-woogie rhyme time of the early 1940's," and Russell Colley, a mechanical engineer who became "the Calvin Klein of space" and was known to a generation of astronauts as the "father of the space suit." There were Rose Hamburger, a 105-year-old racing handicapper; Marion Tinsley, a checker champion unbeaten by man or machine, and a vivacious woman who started out as a showgirl and ended up a princess ("Honeychile Wilder is dead, and if the '21' Club is not in actual mourning, it is because the venerable former speakeasy on West 52nd Street was closed for vacation last week when word got around that one of its most memorable former patrons had died on Aug. 11 at Memorial Sloan-Kettering Cancer Center").

Mr. Thomas, a tall man with wavy hair who spoke in a voice soft with traces of his native Tennessee, was an extremely gregarious and social man. Last week he officiated at the annual New Year's Eve party he first started giving at the family home in Shelbyville 32 years ago. About 5 percent of the town's 12,000 people attended, and Mr. Thomas, wearing a blue silk shirt with embroidered sun and moon that he bought for the occasion, cheered his guests and the new century. As in past years, he expressed hopes that the fireworks he had ordered would not set fire to the Presbyterian church across the road.

He was fond of writing about people who became legendary as a result of a single exploit, like Douglas Corrigan, who took off from New York in a tiny overloaded plane bound for California (he said) in 1938 and landed in Dublin some 28 hours later. He became an instant hero, forever to be known as Wrong Way Corrigan, but in his obituary, Mr. Thomas went beyond recapitulation to suggest that Mr. Corrigan was more cunning than befuddled. He wrote:

"Although he continued to claim with a more or less straight face that he had simply made a wrong turn and been led astray by a faulty compass, the story was far from convincing, especially to the American aviation authorities who had rejected his repeated requests to make just such a flight because his modified 1929 Curtiss-Robin monoplane was judged unworthy."

In a similar vein, he wrote of Johnny Sylvester, who died in 1990, 64 years after he came to fame as a bedridden boy who inspired Babe Ruth. Here is how Mr. Thomas began his obituary, which was included in "The Last Word: The New York Times Book of Obituaries and Farewells" (William Morrow): "There are those who will tell you that little Johnny Sylvester was never that sick and certainly not dying. They will tell you that Babe Ruth never promised to hit a home run for him in Game 4 of the 1926 World Series, and that the three home runs that the Babe did hit in that game in no way saved the 11-year-old youngster's life.

"Any representations to the contrary, these people will tell you, were simply embellishments of a trivial incident by an over-sentimental press in a hypersentimental age.

"Such people are known as cynics."

There was something mythic, too, about Sylvia Weinberger, Mr. Thomas wrote, "who used a sprinkling of matzoh meal, a pinch of salt and a dollop of schmaltzmanship to turn chopped liver into a commercial success."

Robert McGill Thomas Jr. was born and grew up in Shelbyville, Tenn., where chopped liver is rare and schmaltz is not part of the vernacular. He spent his 15th year cheering for a distant relative, Senator Estes Kefauver, as Kefauver ran for vice president on the Democratic ticket with Adlai E. Stevenson. Three years later Mr. Thomas went to Yale, where he worked on the student newspaper and flunked out as a result of a decision, he said, "to major in New York rather than anything academic."

After joining The Times as a copyboy in 1959, Mr. Thomas spent the next four decades in a variety of reporting assignments, often prowling police stations and working the phones in the late hours to produce fast-breaking stories. With his fondness for anomalies, Mr. Thomas might have described his own journalistic career as more circuitous than meteoric.

Always regarded as a stylish writer by his colleagues, he sometimes ran into career turbulence because of an acknowledged tendency to carry things like sentences, paragraphs, ideas and enthusiasms further than at least some editors preferred. Indeed, he went beyond acknowledging this trait to defending it. "Of course I go too far," he used to say. "But unless you go too far how are you ever going to find out how far you can go?"

All of this may explain the sympathy he showed in his obituaries of underachievers and late bloomers.

There was certainly no sense of superiority in his account of the life choice made by Steven Slepack, a man who gave up a promising career in marine biology to become Professor Bendeasy, "the man in the beribboned tuxedo jacket who delighted a generation of schoolchildren by twisting balloons into animals in Central Park." He described a character actor named Jack Weston as "the quintessential New Yorker, which is to say he was born in Cleveland and lived in Los Angeles for 18 years, hating every minute of it he wasn't actually in front of the camera."

In writing about Anton Rosenberg, a painter and jazz musician, Mr. Thomas said he "embodied the Greenwich Village hipster ideal of 1950's cool to such a laid-back degree and with such determined detachment that he never amounted to much of anything."

For some admirers, for whom Mr. Thomas's work came to be known as "McG's," a favorite was his obituary of Edward Lowe, which revealed how Mr. Lowe, a sawdust merchant from Cassopolis, Mich., found a new use for some kiln-dried granulated clay he had been selling as a sop for grease spills in industrial plants and created a million-dollar market for the product he named and marketed as Kitty Litter.

Mr. Thomas provided the antecedent action to the tale in a second paragraph that established the historical significance of Mr. Lowe's achievement: "Cats have been domesticated since ancient Egypt, but until a fateful January day in 1947, those who kept them indoors full time paid a heavy price. For all their vaunted obsession with paw-licking cleanliness, cats, whose constitutions were adapted for arid desert climes, make such an efficient use of water that they produce a highly concentrated urine that is one of the most noxious effluences of the animal kingdom. Boxes filled with sand, sawdust or wood shavings provided a measure of relief from the resulting stench, but not enough to make cats particularly welcome in discriminating homes."

One of his admirers was Joseph Epstein, the literary essayist. "I have noted an interesting general-assignment obituary writer with the somewhat overloaded name of Robert McG. Thomas Jr., who occasionally gets beyond the facts and the rigid formula of the obit to touch on—of all things to find in The New York Times—a deeper truth," Mr. Epstein wrote.

"Thus Thomas on one Fred Rosenstiel, 'who spent his life planting gardens to brighten the lives of his fellow New Yorkers, and to alleviate an abiding sadness in his heart. . . .' The sadness, we learn later in the obituary, derived from Mr. Rosenstiel's inability to 'forgive himself for surviving the Holocaust.' A fine touch."

In addition to his wife, Mr. Thomas is survived by their twin sons, Andrew, of Lewes, Del., and David, of Manhattan; a sister, Carey Gates Thomas Hines, of Birmingham, Ala., and two grandchildren.

January 8, 2000